Muslim
Teenagers
Coping

with parents, family, life,
the universe and everything

Ruqaiyyah Waris Maqsood

Ta-Ha Publishers Ltd
www.taha.co.uk

Second Revised Edition March 2009
Reprinted 2009, 2012

Published by
Ta-Ha Publishers Ltd.
Unit 4, The Windsor Centre
Windsor Grove, West Norwood
London, SE27 9NT, UK
www.tahapublishers.com

By: Ruqaiyyah Waris Maqsood
General Editor: Dr. Abia Afsar-Siddiqui
Edited by: Abdassamad Clarke

Cover/Book Design and Typeset by: Open Squares.co.uk
Printed and Bound by: Imak Ofset, Turkey

A catalogue record of this book is available from the British Library
ISBN-13: 978-1-84200-099-1

Contents

Please say:

ﷺ – *sallallahu alayhi wasallam* (Peace and blessings of Allah be upon him) whenever the Prophet Muhammad's ﷺ name is mentioned.

السلام – *alayhis salaam* (peace be upon him) whenever a prophet's name is mentioned.

رضي الله عنه – *radiallahu anhu* (may Allah be pleased with him) when the name of any of the Companions of the Prophet Muhammad ﷺ is mentioned.

رضي الله عنها – *radiallahu anha* (may Allah be pleased with her) when the name of any of the wives or female Companions of the Prophet Muhammad ﷺ is mentioned.

Problems, Problems

You may not realise this, but you are one of life's most precious treasures, of extreme value, worth more than gold or silver.

What? That sounds good, since nearly everybody in the world picks on you and manages to find fault with just about everything you try to do. How come all those with super-sharp eyes, who never manage to miss the slightest little things you might do too slowly or too quickly or in too slap-dash a manner or in a bad temper, have not noticed this amazing fact of your great value?

We are, of course, talking about your parents, teachers, so-called friends and relatives. Naturally, you know you love them and that they love you, at least you hope that is the case, but they do seem to have this uncanny knack of catching you at your worst. You know the sort of thing. Your mother yells at you to clear up your bedroom while it is still possible to get in through the door. This is not your favourite job, so that you eventually get down to it on a precious Saturday and spend hours hanging up clothes that you never knew you had, discovering long forgotten items of underwear, trying to sort out your CDs and DVDs...this really ought to be appreciated. You know what a tremendous sacrifice you have just made. Then your mother comes around to inspect and unfortunately the only thing she can manage to notice is a totally irrelevant and minute trail of cobweb across the corner of the ceiling, which happened to be the only thing you had missed. It really is uncanny how they do it. It is such a regular feature of mothers (or sometimes fathers) that one might well assume it is one of the laws of nature.

Never mind. You can console yourself with the thought that you are, after all, a valuable treasure. Oh yes? Is there any proof of that? Actually, there is. Simply because you have started to become aware, no matter in how inexpert a fashion, that there is more to life than tidy bedrooms, expensive or trendy clothes, or the ability to fix bikes, or cook meals, or even to speak Arabic, score goals or type a hundred words a minute. These are all creditable things but no matter how many talents you have, it is not these which make you so valuable.

No – it is because you have the potential to become a very happy and enlightened person, full of serenity and joy, beloved of a partner and a blessing to all who come across you. How? Because you have entered, or are entering, the community of Islam; the company of people who obey, and hope for mercy from, Allah.

Being a teenager, of course, is not an easy business. Thankfully, the problems are not permanent – being a teenager does not last forever. They try to tell you that these are the best days of your life. You may find it hard to believe, but they really mean that being at school is wonderful – how ridiculous! To hear them talk, you'd think the good old days when they used to sit in rows without daring to open their mouths, when they were forever getting the cane for one trivial reason or another, when computers didn't exist, were absolute bliss. In those days, instead of bullies, they were all jolly good pals – except that you know they are kidding themselves.

Why do they do it? Parents are always at it, ignoring your quite serious problems and fobbing you off with some nonsense – if you can get them to listen to you at all, that is. Sometimes it feels as if they spend their entire time wishing you would go away and leave them in peace. It hardly seems fair – you didn't ask to be born, did you? If that is their attitude, why did they bother to have you in the first place? They have no right to treat you as if you were just a burden and nuisance, giving deep sighs or laughing you off when you eventually pluck up the courage to tell them something that is really bothering you.

What is the worst thing about being a teenager? Probably the irritation of being "too old" to do half the things you want to do and "too young" to do the other half. Life can seem dismally unfair when you have lived for over thirteen years – there isn't much attraction in being told that you may have sixty more years to go.

Nevertheless, you have arrived at The Awkward Age and have discovered that, in the opinion of your parents, your Awkward Age started the moment you were born (or even before) and is likely to go on until you turn up your toes.

If you are male, you have found that being male poses certain inevitable challenges and places certain inevitable demands upon you. For a start, every female in the universe seems to "get" at you, in one way or another – either to tell you off, laugh at you, make you do something quicker or make you do something you have no desire whatsoever to do. Mothers seem determined to keep young men in "short trousers" refusing to recognise that they are almost men and quite capable of acting in a sensible and responsible manner. Mothers can be positively embarrassing and, when they are over-possessive, make young men look ridiculous among their friends, as if teenagers don't already have enough to contend with.

And if you are a girl, you are beginning to discover how unfair it is that you have been born female – you have to work harder, be more patient, more understanding, more tolerant, more loving, just about more everything than boys. When you have achieved all this, they are still the ones who get all the attention, all the praise, all the fuss made of them. Sometimes, it doesn't seem to matter what you do, nobody is ever going to take any notice or thank you for it – whereas the least little thing your abominable brother does sends them all into ecstasies. As it happens, girls can be pretty good at things like physics and chemistry, or other subjects that people generally consider to be boys' subjects. You might beat your brother hands down, but it is him that they want to send to college and they don't seem to have much interest in the fact that *you* might want to take up an academic career.

Don't even mention putting up with the suffering of "women's problems". You have to grin and bear it, drag yourself off to school when it's your time-of-the-month and feel pretty rotten – but your dear brother can collapse in a heap and get waited on hand and foot over the least little snuffle.

Yes, whether male or female, you can't win. You are beginning to get just a little inkling that things in life don't seem to be quite fair somehow. You are beginning to feel just a bit downtrodden and resentful – and when you have a long cool look at the way things have worked out for people you know who are older than you, it doesn't look as if things are going to be all that much better for you in the future.

Parents seem determined to make young people do all their work for them, refusing to recognise that they need some free time to relax and just be themselves or in which to study. They blow hot and cold – drooling over their "little pets" one minute and being far too strict the next. All your friends go out and about to clubs and parties – but you are never allowed out of their sight. They really don't seem to trust you at all and that's not much of a compliment.

Yes, parents can be a problem, so can friends, teachers, the boss when you start work, relationships with the opposite sex and, of course, your own selves whose deficiencies are only too glaringly obvious to you.

As if all this wasn't bad enough, just when you really need a little morale boosting along come the spots. You suddenly discover that you are far too short, or too tall and thin, or too fat – and there is nothing you can do about it. Your voice might break out in embarrassing squeaks just when you have to read something out loud or answer a question; you always knock something over when you pass through a room. You notice (because your dear classmates have picked on you a thousand times and let you know this bad news but it always hurts more when you hit your teens) that your ears stick out; you realise with a crunch that nobody will *ever* like you because you have to wear bottle-bottom glasses, or that you are no good at sport, or that bullies can wipe the floor with you any time they choose. You discover that you have asthma or hay fever or acne or eczema – and know that you are doomed to a lifetime of pills and potions, with people laughing at you or pointing the finger instead of giving you the sympathy you deserve. Might as well be a fox asking for sympathy from a pack of hounds. In short, there are days when the whole world seems determined to bring you down, as if there were a cosmic conspiracy at work, zooming in with disasters just for you.

There are extra worries. What happens if all your friends have started smoking? You feel left out – what should you do? You may not particularly want to smoke or, on the other hand, you may want to very much but know your parents would go mad if they caught you out. The same thing, of course, would apply if you wanted to go with the gang to a club, not to mention a pub – even if you promised only to drink orange juice.

What happens if the gang gets into more serious stuff – things like taking drugs or sniffing solvents or becoming involved in serious romance? They all seem to be at it and to hear some boys talk, you'd think that nothing in skirts was safe from their irresistible manly advances. Sometimes they are just a laugh but sometimes the way they talk is disgusting. It is not just that they keep up this dirty sniggering all the time but it might one day be you or someone you know that they are talking about. They don't seem to have any idea whatsoever that girls are individuals who just might genuinely have character and sensitive feelings.

Then, on top of all this, your parents never stop getting at you about their religion. Your father may be one of these types who really hasn't got time to do anything for his family, either your mother or you, because he's all the time on his knees saying his prayers or he's scooted off down to the mosque for hours on end. You hardly see the man – he doesn't seem to allow any time for "ordinary life" or the people who have a claim on his time and affections – surely he's overdoing it? Whether Allah is pleased with all his attention or not, you know his time with you leaves a lot to be desired and you can't help being just a little bit resentful. No wonder your mother was always going on at him but now she has given up and crept "off the pitch", lonely, misunderstood and defeated.

Now, of course, that you are into your teens, he is beginning to lean heavily on you. It is just about the only thing he ever notices about you – that you regard his way of life as "Stone Age" and totally irrelevant, yet he expects you to follow in his footsteps and enjoy the same things. You can think of nothing more boring than spending hours listening to religious talks or studying religious rules and regulations when you'd really rather be playing football, gossiping with the gang, getting in the Mercedes, going cross-eyed on the latest computer-game or even doing your homework. Some of your friends really do go to clubs and pubs. If your father knew you even considered mixing with them, he'd just go crazy.

Somehow or other, he seems to have lived his entire life without ever feeling the urge to enjoy himself. You almost think he's a dead stick and you have made up your mind that the last thing you want to do is end up like him or your mother. The business of humouring your parents just enough so that they leave you alone is becoming more of a balancing act each day, increasing in direct proportion to the number of things you want to do that they have never heard of, or if they had, they would certainly disapprove of. The strain of it is beginning to tell and patience and tempers on both sides are shortening. The air is thick with rows. It is all getting beyond a joke.

No wonder you are getting rebellious. It's not that you are against anybody's religion and you are not asking your parents to give up anything they enjoy doing – but is it reasonable that they should be trying to "live their lives again" through you? You are different people entirely, the world has moved on and your parents ought to realise that, yet they just go on trying to make you carbon copies of themselves.

What is more, you all know from watching what happens to older friends, that when things really come to a head, when you're around sixteen or so, that some of them just give up trying. Parents go all stiff and tight-lipped and their children have just had enough and can't cope with any more of it and "drop out".

In some families there is the added dread that your parents might marry you off to some awful person you haven't even met. You hear horror stories of girls and boys being taken "back home" to "have a nice holiday" and meet their relatives – and then they don't come back.

Your parents seem determined not to let you choose your own marriage partners, but on the other hand, they seem equally determined to marry you off as soon as possible. That's not very complimentary either – it makes it seem as if they are just trying to get rid of you at all costs. Getting them to listen to you and have confidence in you is a problem, indeed. They come on far too "heavy".

Some of the students you have seen at school have really ended up on the heap, going from truancy to hanging about on the criminal fringe, to being involved in crime, to ending up unemployed and unhappy, possibly even pregnant before marriage (and/or having abortions) or on drugs. When you think about it seriously, it's really very sad. Somebody ought to have loved those young people and helped them make it through – but their parents either just didn't seem to bother or they leaned on them too hard or they weren't strong enough themselves to cope. In a few ghastly cases you know of, there was physical abuse and trouble; desperate fathers beating their daughters or locking them up and not allowing them out. It didn't work – it just caused more heartache. Newspapers have even reported a few cases of Muslim men killing their daughters who disappointed them or whom they felt had "shamed" them.

If your family is OK, all this may seem to belong to another world and another time but you know it happens and it's frightening.

It's a mess. Why on earth should they expect you to be religious at all when, very likely, if anyone is to blame, it must be God? When all is said and done, they believe that God is really in charge of everything; they keep telling you that nothing can happen without it being His will. So, if you end up being an idiot or a drug addict, that must be His will too, mustn't it? So it's obviously all God's fault, if there really is a God – and yet they still want you to get down on your knees five times a day and get up while it's still dark and fast one month per year, just to please this Almighty Being that no-one has conclusively proved to exist and that certainly doesn't seem to have done a single thing to help you or your pals.

What kind of deal is that?

When you think about it – what about all those starving people in the Third World or those poor souls that get washed away in floods or buried in earthquakes or massacred in wars that they certainly didn't cause or want? Funny sort of God – to allow all that to happen and still expect people to love and serve Him.

It's all a great big question...WHY? You are not philosophers; you are not the brains of the universe. You are just children struggling not to get fat, coping with spots and you haven't done your homework and you've forgotten to wash your PE kit and your mother is nagging you to pray again... You are not sure if it's everyone else that's going mental or you.

In other words – HELP! If there *is* somebody there – please look this way for a second and spare a thought for *us*!

Does GodExist?

Well, does God really exist? Is there a God or isn't there? That has to be the one that really counts. Problems, problems – because if there isn't, you can probably forget the rest.

Despite the millions of gallons of ink humanity have spilled arguing over this, it really is a blindingly simple choice. The choice is only one of two – either there is a God or there isn't. If there isn't, you can forget everything about life after death, rewards and punishments for the way you live your life, the quaint notion that somewhere inside you there is a "conscience" that tells you what you ought to do, that you have a soul. If there isn't a God, that's all just wishful thinking or a crude attempt by certain people in authority to make others do what they want.

On the other hand, if there *is* a God, you have to face the lot. Obviously, adults can't expect you to grasp it all in five minutes; you know perfectly well that intelligent people have grappled with the problems of theology all their lives and the honest ones still admit that they don't know all the answers. Some people seem to believe all sorts of clap-trap that you know perfectly well goes completely against what scientists have discovered about the universe. Others have done a reasonable job of reconciling true scientific discovery with their belief in God but it's a hard job for you to sort out what is reasonable and what is just superstition. If the Qur'an is true, God has provided Himself with a very neat little "let-out clause".[1] God's "let-out clause" is to state categorically that the universe is full of things that you have no knowledge of, that you simply cannot know and that He is so far above and beyond your sphere of understanding and experience, that even the greatest brains in the world can never fully understand Him.

"No vision grasps Him, but He grasps all vision; and He is the Subtle (above all comprehension), the All-Aware (Who is acquainted with all things)." (Surah Al-An'am 6:103)

"Allah, there is no god but He, the Living, the Eternal. Neither slumber nor sleep takes Him. ...And they do not encompass anything of His knowledge except as He wills." (Surah Al-Baqara 2:255)

---

1 "Let-out clause" is an expression meaning that no matter what you do or how you think things out, you will never be able to prove something because there's always a "let-out". A perfect example is people who talk about death-bed experiences; if the supposedly dead really survived and lived to tell the tale, it would be impossible to prove that they had truly been dead. See what I mean?

Well, that's great news. We can never understand Him. So why should anyone in their right mind believe in Him?

There are several reasons. Allah is Perfect Justice. If there is a Day of Judgement, a time when people will be rewarded or punished for the way they have lived their lives, then God would not be fair at all if He didn't let people know what they were supposed to do and not do. God could not blame you for not doing what He wants, if He didn't tell you what He wants. That would not be Perfect Justice at all but blatantly unfair.

IF God exists, He must have revealed something about Himself for people to study and understand. He must have left some kind of "rule of life" for people to follow. Otherwise, if there is no eternity to worry about, you might as well get on with doing what you enjoy doing and forget worrying. If there is Nobody watching, what does it matter what you do? You don't usually go round doing deliberately nasty things; you don't usually deliberately want to hurt or upset people. That these things sometimes happen to you is not really your fault – they just happen. Everyone suffers from misunderstandings, don't they?

Well, of course they do. There is one thing that all spiritual, reflective, thinking people who have become aware of God, do insist on as part of God's relationship with you. They insist that God is Perfectly Fair and that therefore He has sent revelations to human beings in every generation. There have always been "people of insight" who were able to "see" or understand a bit more about Allah than everyone else and it was their duty to share with everyone else what Allah "reveals" that He wants or expects them to do.

Allah never forces people to do anything – except you could almost say He "forced" these special people to be "Revealers" or "Messengers". At least, once they had taken hold of their insight, they were never able to put the subject down. It took over their entire lives and influenced thousands of other people to accept what they taught.

Well, you might say – what about my generation? Where is the special prophet telling *us* what to do? There seem to be so many different religions and they all think they are right and the others are wrong. Who will tell you the truth? Can God really blame you if you can't make up your mind or if you finally decide that each one is as good as the other so it doesn't matter which one you choose or that none of them really matter at all, so long as you do your best to be a "good guy"?

Now you come to the first serious decision in being a Muslim. Each religion tells you what it thinks is right; you can probably safely assume that the best people in each religion are honest and deeply believe in what they say. Therefore, you can certainly make the same assumption for the religion of Islam and see if you can work out what makes Muslims tick and why they believe the things they do. The statement of belief of a Muslim is extremely simple but at the same time, the most amazingly difficult and complex thing in the world. On the one hand, it is so simple that any person who has reached the age of reason can grasp it, but it is so difficult that it keeps the most intelligent brains in the world going for the whole of their lives.

It is this:

$$\text{لَآ إِلَهَ إِلاَّ اللهُ مُحَمَّدٌ رَسُولُ اللهِ}$$

La ilaha illallah Muhammad ar-rasulallah
There is no god but Allah, Muhammad is the Messenger of Allah

In other words – Allah *is* and Muhammad ﷺ (who lived over a thousand years ago) is the Prophet and Messenger for your generation as well as the one he lived in. That's all there is to it? Yes, but …

"There is no god but Allah" implies a million things. First, it states that there really is a God. That is the first acceptance. It all starts with what Muslims call *ihsan* which means "the making something excellent, good and beautiful". Let us find out what that means by exploring first the word "realisation". Realisation is the heart of the whole matter and can begin even when faith – or even the possibility of faith – is very weak. No leader or teacher in the world can *make* it happen, although they might do their best to guide people towards Allah. Sometimes, because of the nature of human weakness and failings, the teacher's best is not good enough or is not convincing. That doesn't make any difference.

One of the most important of Allah's statements is that **"Truth stands out clearly from error,"** (Surah Al-Baqara

2:256). If a thing is true, it doesn't matter what nonsense people talk about it – it will in the beginning or the end be self-evident and people, when they reason, will either come to it or deliberately choose to ignore it. Already, do you see, once you begin to grasp that there is such a thing as Truth, then it is clear that there has to be such a thing as Judgement.

You cannot be forced to feel faith any more than you can be forced to feel love. It is a matter of awareness. One minute there may be nothing there at all, you are ambling along your way whistling nonchalantly, the sky is blue, the birds are singing; then – Wham! The whole universe suddenly changes and you become both the most important and enlightened being in the world because of your flash of insight and at the same time the most minute and insignificant speck of dust.

You suddenly become aware of His "Presence" and – well, you don't know the word for it, but He is beyond everything, holding the entire universe in the "palm of His hand", knowing everything, even the number of hairs on your head and your innermost secret thoughts; you want to crumple up before this intense and searing knowledge that you never realised before or you feel the most incredible wave of feeling that you can't explain, something moving in the depth of your heart, an overwhelming joy and gratitude and amazement that out of all the millions of things that exist Allah sees *you* and cares about *you*. He can see everything that you have gone through and is merciful to you. Even when you felt you were most alone, you can suddenly see now that you were not alone at all but that Allah was with you. You have heard about people who suddenly discover God exists, bursting into tears and thought how ridiculous that was – but now, all of a sudden, you want to sing and cry at the same time. It doesn't always have to happen like that, in fact it never happens the same to two different people. But this is nothing new. The acute realisation that Allah knows you, watches you and cares for you is one that has brought tougher men and women than you to their knees.

The second part of the statement of faith is that Muhammad ﷺ genuinely is the Messenger of Allah. What does this mean? It means that around two thousand years after the Prophet Musa ﷺ and six hundred years or so after the Prophet Isa ﷺ, another man was called and set apart by Allah to reveal His message and this man was an Arab of the Quraysh tribe, born at Makkah in Arabia.

How can you know he was a genuine Prophet and Messenger of Allah? The fact is you can't, if you want it in the sense of academic proof and exposition, but you do know. This is why the second part of the Muslim statement is also an act of faith, faith that you do know what you know. Muslims declare that they believe 100% in the genuine prophetic calling of Muhammad ﷺ and that the message revealed through him confirms everything that Allah revealed to humanity before and supersedes and replaces it.

This brings you to a third item for a Muslim, one that is the cause of the whole business. The revealed message that Muhammad ﷺ received and passed on is available for you to read and study for yourself – the Noble Qur'an. Since Muslims accept that this *is* the revealed message of Allah, you are inevitably bound to accept what it says – even if some of the messages are surprising or at first uncomfortable to you or do not quite fit in with what people would like.

A person becoming a Muslim has no choice in the matter – if you believe Allah is Real and Muhammad ﷺ is a Prophet whom Allah truly made revelation to, then the words revealed, i.e. the Qur'an, *are* the genuine message from Allah and all one can do is reject them or submit to them. One of the important statements in the Qur'an is that Muhammad ﷺ is the last prophet because the words revealed in the Qur'an are the full unadulterated message of Allah, which have endured unaltered for almost a millennium and a half and will continue so until the end of time.

> **"The revelation of the Book in which there is no doubt is from the Lord of all created beings. Or do they say: 'He has forged it'? No, it is the Truth from your Lord so that you might warn a people to whom no warner had come before you, so they might be guided."**
> (Surah As-Sajda 32:1-3)

The word "Muslim" means "someone who submits" – a person who makes a conscious decision to put their will second to Allah's, insofar as they can understand Allah's will through the Qur'an and the *sunnah,* the way of the Prophet Muhammad ﷺ.

A Muslim is not a *Muhammadan*. Muslims are not people who worship Muhammad. That is complete nonsense – even though you love Muhammad ﷺ, cherish the stories about him and study his own sayings and way of life. The Qur'an itself makes it very clear that worship of a prophet or an angel or any being or thing as if he was God Himself, or part of God, is such a crass misunderstanding of the indivisible nature of Allah that the worshipper has demonstrated complete unawareness of the true nature of God.

"Allah is the One Who created you, then provided for you, then will cause you to die and then will raise you to life. Are there any of your "partners" who can do anything of that? Glory be to Him! High is He above that which they associate (as His partners)."
(Surah Ar-Rum 30:40)

"Behold! Whoever is in the heavens and whoever is in the earth belong to Allah. What do they follow, the ones who call on less-than-Allah as partners? They only follow opinion. They do nothing but lie."
(Surah Yunus 10:66)

Believing that Allah has partners or is somehow made up of separate aspects or entities is the wrong action Muslims call *shirk* – which does not mean "to avoid work" (the meaning of an English word which resembles exactly the Arabic word), but to "share in" an aspect of Divinity. It is the error of the Christians, who, out of intense misdirected piety and devotion, have misunderstood the true Compassion of the One God and have elevated their prophet, Jesus, to the status of Godhead.

If you are claiming to be a Muslim then you have to face these three challenges:

1) Do you really and genuinely trust in your heart that Allah exists and is aware of you and knows everything that you do and think?

2) Do you really trust that Muhammad ﷺ is Allah's genuine prophet (and since it says so as part of the revelation, that he is the *last* prophet)?

3) Do you really trust that the Qur'an is Allah's direct message to you (yes to you!) revealed to Muhammad ﷺ for him to pass on to all humanity in order for you all to pass the tests of life and earn eternal reward and not damnation or failure?

You may have grown up all your life in a Muslim family but if you have never really accepted these challenges in your heart, then you are not yet truly a Muslim! You may be familiar with the ideas but you have to trust them for yourself. Nobody can do it for you – it doesn't work like that.

So, you have just arrived at the "age of reason". You are beginning to question things and starting to search through the darkness for something that makes sense of the universe. The time has come for you to sit down and try to fathom what you believe or why you don't accept any of the three challenges raised in this chapter.

If you can make out a reasonable case for why you don't, then perhaps you will be able to start seriously working out the alternatives and it may be that, if there are no serious alternatives, Allah will begin to move you in His direction.

Think for a minute about ants. Look at them running around in the garden, busy little things, so occupied with their chores and duties, completely unaware that you exist. You could pick one up – it still would not be able to "see" you; you are a creature far too vast and you inhabit a completely different universe from his. We are ants too, running around hither and thither, completely unaware of the All-Seeingness of the Eternal Watcher – until the moment He chooses to stop us in our tracks and make us see. Unlike the ant, we can choose to seek Him out.

> **"Allah. There is no god but He, the Living, the Self-Subsisting Eternal. Neither slumber nor sleep take Him. Everything in the heavens and on earth is His. Who intercedes in His presence except as He gives permission? He knows what went before them and what comes after them. And they do not encompass anything of His knowledge except as He wills. His throne extends over the heavens and the earth, and it does not weary Him to guard and preserve them; and He is the High, the Supreme in Glory."** (Surah Al-Baqara 2:255)

Testing, Testing

People who are Muslims just cannot pass their lives without bearing in mind the eternal consequences of their beliefs and actions. We trust Allah's statement that everything we do is known to Him – every thought, every inclination, every motive.

> **"And know that Allah has full knowledge of everything."** (Surah Al-Baqara 2:231)

> **"Allah has full knowledge of the very inmost thoughts of the breasts."** (Surah Al-Ma'ida 5:7)

This is not an easy matter to take seriously when you are a teenager – you think you have years ahead of you to live and enjoy and you can worry about all this kind of thing later. It is, however, a vital part of the revelation and it has to be understood by every human, including teenagers and, although it is always difficult to "place old heads on young shoulders", the moment you arrive at the "age of reason" it is important that you understand this attribute of Allah quite clearly – because it gives the point to your entire life.

Islam teaches that the reason for living is not just for you to wander aimlessly about, enjoying yourself as best you can. It is to pass a test. Therefore, it stands to reason that not every part of our lives is going to be pleasant or easy. Tests never are.

You are not forced to believe any of this, of course – that is a matter entirely up to you, but all caring adult Muslims (and teenagers, for all intents and purposes, are adults) have a duty to take the chance to know the evidence, so that they can consider the facts for themselves and choose the right path, if Allah wills.

If a Know-All God merely observed us for the sole purpose of bringing us down (and don't we all know people who are just like this – only too delighted when we do something wrong or look silly) – then our Lord Allah would *not* be The Compassionate, The Merciful One, but a rather malicious despot, laughing at our troubles and mishaps and enjoying the spectacle of seeing us get into difficulties. We do not like our fellow humans when they are like this; if they are people who have power over us, who are able to hurt and punish us for the things we get wrong, we then consider them to be nasty and despicable tyrants, against whom it would be perfectly justifiable to rebel.

So, where does this leave our image of Allah? What exactly is this test all about and why do *any* people get punished at all?

The Qur'an reveals two things:
- Firstly, that Allah is not a wishy-washy acceptor of any kind of conduct or morality, Who will softly let pass people who deliberately and callously hurt and damage others or who live egotistical selfish lives;
- Secondly, that although it is Allah who punishes these people, they really bring it upon themselves.

> **"Truly Allah is severe in punishment."**
> (Surah Al-Ma'ida 5:2 and see also Surah Al-Baqara 2:196)

> **"Rather, man will be a witness against himself, even though he offers his excuses."**
> (Surah Al-Qiyama 75:14-15)

Although Allah will, in due course, punish certain people, it is never His wish to have to punish them. If you study Allah's Beautiful Names you discover that He is *Al-Ghaffar* (The Repeatedly Forgiving) and *Al-Barr* (The Source of All Goodness). The Qur'an teaches that any people who repent and turn back to Allah and make some effort to put right the things they have done wrong, find forgiveness straight away.

Nobody is perfect; we have all done things of which we are ashamed. If Allah punished us according to what we really deserved, then He would leave no-one unpunished. He says, **"If Allah were to take mankind to task for that which they have earned He would not have left on its (the earth's) surface a single living creature."** (Surah Fatir 35:45). The Qur'an teaches that people who return to Allah need not grieve or fear, but those who insist on turning their backs on Him and behaving badly will be responsible for punishing themselves.

> **"And Allah does not wrong them, but they wrong themselves."** (Surah Al 'Imran 3:117)

Allah is also *Al-Qadir* (The Powerful) and *Al-Wali* (The Protecting Friend). You shall certainly be tested – that is the reason for your life; but it is not Allah's wish for you to fail.

It would hardly be reasonable for Allah to place you in situations that are intolerable for you and then expect you to be successful. That would make Him God the Very Unfair. No, He has promised you that He will place no trial or burden on you that is really beyond your capacity – nothing that you should not be able to bear. Therefore, the tests and trials are not unreasonable, even if you may think they are at the time you are going through them.

"And We will definitely test you with somewhat of fear and hunger and loss of goods and lives and fruits (of your actions); and give good news to those who patiently persevere, who when afflicted by a calamity said: 'Truly you belong to Allah, and truly you are returning to Him.'"
(Surah Al-Baqara 2:155-156)

Why does Allah want to test you? It is not because He wants to see how firm your trust is, whether you turn away from Him after some disaster happens to you or whether you remain calm and steadfast. He wants to improve you, make you grow out of your weaknesses and selfishness.

In the world of the Beyond, which you cannot see, Allah created beings with no feelings or free will as humans have. They always do the right things because they have no choice. When Allah created humans, He did something different – He made us out of humble material but He gave us free will. That means that you are capable of choice and discernment; it also means that you are capable of being morally superior even to the angels.

It also means, of course, that you are capable of making the wrong choices. You are free to make the most shattering decision of all – you can choose to reject Allah, your Maker, and Allah will not prevent you.

However, when the Day comes when all the souls return and stand before Him for Judgement, life as you know it here will have already ceased to be and then Allah Himself will make His choice – of those who have passed and those who have failed their tests.

> "This is what you are promised, for every one who turns in sincere repentance, and is a guardian (of Allah's commands and prohibitions), who feared the All-Merciful while unseen (by people) and came with a penitent heart." (Surah Qaf 50:32–33)

> "Truly, We give life and death, and to Us is the final goal." (Surah Qaf 50:43)

That is one good reason why our lives here sometimes pass in hard conditions. There is a famous story of a farmer in Africa who grew hemp. He had to grow it in terrible conditions, back-breaking soil with little rain to nourish it. When he moved to a more easy-going climate he took some hemp plants with him, thinking how easily they would grow in these new conditions. Yes, they grew – huge, lush green plants, but when he opened up the stems to take out the fibre – there was nothing there but pulp. The hemp needed the harsh conditions in which to develop backbone. See what I mean? The true Muslim learns to thank Allah even for the hard conditions.

"You enter Islam by saying *Shahadah* (bearing witness). But you can live Islam only by constantly doing *Shahadah*. Doing *Shahadah* will bring you in ceaseless confrontation with false gods inside you and with those outside you. It will also require a ceaseless striving to reshape self and society so as to attest to your witnessing."[2]

Awareness of Allah is a precious gift – but to keep it, to grow in it and derive full benefit from it, certain conditions are necessary. If faith was just doled out to everybody it would become cheap and valueless. It is a precious treasure and you only gain as much of it as you earn.

> **"And that there is nothing for man except that which he has striven for."** (Surah An-Najm 53:39)

Firstly, you may not be granted a blinding flash of inspiration from heaven – you are just an ordinary person, not a pious celebrity. Trust in Allah might not come to you automatically as a gift. You may have to look for it, search for it, struggle to keep it in sight. Many people do not appear to have religious awareness – they do not "see the light" but spend most of their lives blundering about in the dark. Once someone in that darkness spots the gleam of light, no matter how distant, it is stupid not to try to draw close and walk in it.

Allah does not shift about and change ground. You can be sure that if you genuinely start to look for Him with conscious effort, you will find that the way to Him is a straight path.

---

2   Khurram Murad, *Sacrifice*, The Islamic Foundation, 1985, p.5

Because of your free will He will not make you see that path; He only guides you if you turn yourself round and watch for the signs that will take you along it.

> **"And He guides to Himself whoever turns in penitence."** (Surah Ash-Shura 42:13)

> **"And the ones who strive for Us, We will definitely guide them in Our paths."** (Surah Al-Ankabut 29:69)

The purpose and meaning of life for a Muslim is always to strive to seek Allah's pleasure, to live and to die in His way. People without awareness of Allah live only on the level of the animal kingdom – eating, drinking, procreating and dying and have not really taken on the responsibility of being human. Really, there is little point to some people's lives, as they themselves will often admit, especially when they become depressed. But those who have awareness of Allah are also aware of eternity and their existence is meaningful.

"Life is thus lifted up from being a transient, fleeting moment in history, terminable at death, to an eternal event. Our existence is no more directed to merely coveting and acquiring the blessings and bounties that abound in this world. Instead the way is open to turn this world's possessions into everlasting benefits to be reaped in that world, sometimes by taking and enjoying them, gratefully, sometimes by giving them up."[3]

---

3 *Ibid.*, pg. 8

We cannot do it by mere wishful thinking. It is not enough to make claims and statements of belief – we have to live the Way. Just as we achieve absolutely nothing in this life without personal effort, so we may have to struggle hard to prove we are worthy of the life to come.

> **"Rather, did you think that you would enter the Garden while Allah did not yet know the ones who struggled of you, and so He might know the patient ones?"** (Surah Al 'Imran 3:142)

> **"Do people think they will be left because they say: 'We believe' and they will not be put to the test? We certainly tested the ones before them."** (Surah Al-Ankabut 29:2-3)

Sacrifice
Please Readjust
Your Mind

"My prayer and my sacrifice, my living and my dying, all belong to Allah, the Lord of all the creatures." (Surah Al-An'am 6:162)

The bad news is that life, for a Muslim, can be a constant stream of sacrifices. The good news is that when you are in love with someone, nothing is too much trouble. You would do absolutely anything, go to any lengths to please the beloved. If you have not yet been in love, you simply have to observe the behaviour of people you know who are.

Muslims are in love with Allah or they are in the process of imitating love, so that they might catch fire and really fall in love. It is not like human love for each other, of course, but unless we Muslims feel this burning devotion and commitment to Allah in the very depths of our hearts and souls, we will find it very hard to be successful in the life of total commitment that Allah requires of us.

"And the ones who believe are stronger in their love for Allah." (Surah Al-Baqara 2:165)

Put another way, those who love Allah believe that nothing is too worthy or too valuable to sacrifice to earn Allah's pleasure. Giving something up only deserves the name sacrifice if we love and value it. These things usually include our time, money, worldly possessions, physical abilities and might even include life itself. Other things we are called on to sacrifice if we are trying to live as Muslims might be our ties of love and affection, likes or dislikes, preferences and prejudices, views and opinions, pleasures and comforts, status and roles.

However, there is really only one principle behind the lot – when we give anything away for the sake of Allah, what we really give up is not the object or thing in itself, but our loving it before our love of Allah.

Why we sacrifice these things is perfectly reasonable and logical and not based on a perverted desire for asceticism (self-denial) or for the wrong motive of wishing others to think us pious. We only give up something we love and to which we attach value because we have found something we love more and to which we attach greater value.

Every adult human being (remember we have included teenagers among the adults because we don't wish to be counted among the children) knows what it is to make sacrifices. Ordinary everyday social life is based upon them. Without people making sacrifices there would be no peace, harmony or co-operation and human beings would be in a state of total self-centredness, resulting in constant conflict and misery.

Anyone who has eyes sees the results of selfish living all around them when people are not prepared to make sacrifices. Some people certainly seem to care about nothing except for the gratification of their own desires. This is only compatible with Islam when our desires are no longer for ourselves but for doing the will of Allah, our Lord.

Atheists (people who don't believe in or trust God) just cannot understand this and that is why they are so often unhappy people.

The grace that flows from Allah can be compared to a supply of electricity flowing through equipment that is plugged in. The soul of an atheist is separated from its original source, that is, from its connection with Allah, because of distrust. When this connection is severed, sadness, misery and distress become a permanent part of that person's life. The grace of Allah is not reaching them. After all, is it possible to get the supply of electricity after turning off at the mains?

> **"It is only through the remembrance of Allah that hearts become tranquil."** (Surah Ar-Ra'd 13:28)

True Muslims have to permanently adjust their attitudes to themselves, their families and everything they love and enjoy in life.

> "O Allah, I ask of You, Your love, the love of those who love You, and the doing of deeds which may bring Your love to me. Make my love for You greater than my love for myself, for my wealth, for my family, and for cold water." (Hadith of at-Tirmidhi and al-Hakim)

We have to consider the valuable things of our lives from a different point of view. For example, Time is probably our most precious commodity – although it is hard for us to realise this. When we are around fourteen years old, we seem to have been alive a very long time; the teenage years seem to last forever – particularly when your parents are trying to stop you from doing something you want to do because you are too young. When you are sixty-four and looking back at it all, they say those years seemed to have passed in a flash.

Time is the first thing Allah demands of us – but what you are sacrificing is not the Time itself but the way you spend your Time.

"Remember that Time is one thing you cannot hold on to, even for a moment. It must continuously slip away from you, in whatever way you choose to spend it. Its value to you is simply what you gain from it. Time will melt away, what you earn will stay."[4]

Therefore, you have to think about what you are doing, how you are living. Are you wasting your Time? Are you doing

4   *Ibid.*, pg.14

things that you will later regret? If it is true that all your deeds and motives for doing them are "written in your book", how will your book read when it is opened?

Secondly, what about Money? The world is not evil – Allah made it and expects us to be in it, care for and look after it. Our lives in this world are the means by which we gain the right to the next world. Where people go wrong is in making the means into the ends of their lives. Instead of having the goal of eternity, you limit yourself to trying to gain pleasure and satisfaction from this world's things, in this world alone.

> "There has been made to seem fair to mankind the love of appetites, women and children, heaped up hoards of gold and silver, branded horses, cattle, and well-tilled land. That is the enjoyment of the worldly life. And Allah, with Him is the best place of return. Say: 'Shall I inform you of better than that?' For the ones who fear and obey (Allah), with their Lord there are Gardens, with rivers flowing from underneath them, abiding in them, and purified spouses, and the good pleasure of Allah. ..." (Surah Al 'Imran 3:14-15)

It is not easy for you to give up your craving for the pleasures of this world – but remember that if you see as a Muslim sees, you know that nothing really belongs to you. Everything is Allah's and when you sacrifice something for His sake, you are really only returning it to its Rightful Owner.

Also, remember that no material things are of ultimate value – no matter how much you may wish to cling to them, they become nothing when you breathe your last breath. However, the good news is that when you give away or give up something you value or enjoy for the sake of Allah, you will receive it back, increased out of all expected proportion.

> **"Lend to Allah a goodly loan. Whatever you advance, of good, for your selves you will find it with Allah, better and vaster as a reward. And seek the forgiveness of Allah. Truly Allah is All–Forgiving, Compassionate."**
> (Surah Al-Muzzammil 73:20 and see also Surah Al-Baqara 2:245)

If you look on your sacrifices as "deposits" sent on in advance, then the things you know you should give up may not seem so difficult to give up after all. In a way, you could say that you are really giving everything back to yourself – because Allah says that whatever you give is just a "loan" to Him. If your ultimate prosperity lies in submission to the will of Allah, then your sacrifices to Him can only bring you to success in this life and the life to come. Therefore, you should be grateful to be given the opportunity to sacrifice and the ability to offer yourself and your treasured things to Him. What you are really giving up is your "self-will". You do not have to annihilate it, as some people sometimes teach but if you are a Muslim, you have to surrender it to the Will of Allah.

idealism
The Importance of Bricks

All the time you are alive you are developing your own backbone. Sometimes you feel there is no point in trying because you are so small and unimportant that nothing you do will ever matter. But you realise this is quite wrong. It *does* matter. Allah doesn't care whether you are little or weak or of no importance in the world. He knows all about that. What matters to Allah is what you *do* with yourself. And if you join with others who are of like mind, by His grace you may no longer be little and weak.

"How many a little band has overcome a great band by Allah's leave. And Allah is with the steadfast." (Surah Al-Baqara 2:249)

Remember, if you are in total darkness and you strike a match, it is only a little flame but it breaks through and sheds light. And if there are thousands of you with matches making little flames, then how great is the light.

We are like bricks for Allah – bricks, as you know, are boring little non-entities made out of mud – but a wall cannot be made without them. Even the Great Wall of China was put there brick by brick. Although we cannot realise our own importance to Allah or fully know His will for us, we are the bricks of which the Muslim community is made and every one of us has a place. Take that brick away and there is a gaping hole.

> "Truly Allah loves the ones who fight in His way, arrayed in ranks, as if they were a building which is firmly and compactly cemented." (Surah As-Saff 61:4)

If you are a Muslim you cannot just assume that other people will do everything for you. You have a duty to become a responsible adult as soon as you possibly can. It is no use waiting for someone else to take the lead and tell you what to do. If you open your eyes and take a good look at the adults around you and those responsible for governing your small area and then the larger areas – countries and nations – you realise straight away how very wrong so many things are.

The world is not only the place where you live, it is also a battlefield and the enemy is not a person you can see and point the finger at, it is *Shaytan*, the slinking whisperer. He is no simpleton, but the cleverest, most cunning of tricksters, eager to pull unsuspecting people into his clutches.

Two of the most used tricks are to influence people to stop believing in Allah (this is where Science is so often used, you've heard the phrase "Blinding with science") and to make people give in to laziness.

> **The Prophet ﷺ said that he had seen nothing more fearful than Hell, but those wishing to avoid it were sleeping; and he had not seen anything more pleasant than Paradise, but those wishing to gain it were sleeping.** (Hadith of at-Tirmidhi)

Muslims have a massive task – to promote values for as long as they live; to strive to overcome evil, oppression, racism, corruption, misery and replace these with justice, truth, harmony, brotherhood and compassion. It is no good waiting for your elders and betters to do this for you – they are becoming older and waiting for you to grow up and take over.

The moment you realise the existence of Allah, then the responsibility to become a *khalifah* (deputy) is yours.

You can see for yourself how the older generation has certainly not managed to create a perfect world or even a perfect Muslim community. Much of the Muslim community lacks discipline, sound knowledge and often has no sense of *nadhm* (organisation). There is no such thing anywhere in the world as a truly Muslim government. Weakness and corruption and misunderstandings are to be observed everywhere you look.

There is a lot of work to be done and once you have been granted *taqwa* (the conscious awareness of Allah which will prompt you to fearfully obey His commands and prohibitions), you can no longer sit there and wait for someone else to do it.

> **"Struggle for Allah as He ought to be striven for. He chose you. And He did not place upon you in the matter of the Deen any hardship; the way of your father Abraham. He named you "Muslims" before. ... And hold fast to Allah. He is your Protecting Friend; how blessed a Protecting Friend, and how blessed a Helper."**
> (Surah Al-Hajj 22:78)

One of the most important contributions made to humanity by young people is their powerful sense of right and wrong, of fairness, justice and injustice. They are not bogged down by the complications of politics and vested interests. They often see straight into the heart of the matter. And what they see is not always comfortable or acceptable to a lazy and cynical older generation. As you grow older, your family, friends, work, your situation and, above all, your appetites for power, position and accumulation of things, will all grind away to tear down your values – but if you are truly a Muslim you will stand firm and not compromise those things over which you do have control.

"**And the ones who strive for Us, We will definitely guide them in Our paths. And truly, Allah is definitely with the ones who act excellently well (act with** *Ihsan*)." (Surah Al-Ankabut 29:68)

"**And that there is nothing for man except that which he has striven for; and that his endeavour will be seen; then he will be recompensed for it with the fullest recompense; and that to your Lord is the ultimate end.**" (Surah An-Najm 53:39-42)

forbidden Things
Haram foods, drinks and substances

Getting back to the matter of sacrifice, what are the things you are supposed to be sacrificing? Top of the list for Muslims come some of the most luridly promoted and dressed-up-to-be-attractive temptations of all – alcohol, drugs, sex outside of marriage and *haram* foods. All these things are banned to a Muslim and all are highly attractive to young people and readily available in modern society.

If you are the sort of person, like many of us, who is rather weak when it comes to saying "no" to things you know you should not have, then there is bound to be a clash between you and your conscience. This is not to say that you will not be able to end up an excellent Muslim – very often the people who have given in to temptations but then realised their foolishness and found the strength to overcome them, are a thousand times stronger and more genuine than those who have never known temptation. Don't allow yourself to take these words of mine as a licence to submit to whatever temptation you like, however, with the intention of overcoming them later, for later might never come.

There is a story about two angels. These beings had no free will and were quite incapable of doing anything wrong. When Allah heard them tuttutting about the sins that humans commit, He sent them down to earth to try it out for themselves. In one night they saw a woman that they desired, got drunk on alcohol, murdered the woman's guardian and engaged in sex with her. In other words, it is easy to criticise others when you have never known what it is to be tempted. The world is full of self-righteous people whose piety is like this. They are a bit hypocritical, for one truly knows one's own strength and what one would do when one has faced temptation and beaten it.

Now, the laws given by Allah for the guidance of humanity are moral and spiritual principles just as vital and binding as the natural laws of the physical universe and just as certain in the way they work. They are never whimsical or arbitrary but are the result of His infinite knowledge of what is for the good of His creation.

There is a simple guideline to Islam – how to know what to do and what not to do or what is right and wrong – it is to realise that Allah has permitted everything that is beneficial to humanity and prohibited everything which is harmful. Harmful things for Muslims are any things which degrade them, lower their dignity as human beings, or hurt their body, mind or soul, or are injurious to society as a whole. In other words, Islam is kindly common-sense. If it doesn't hurt or degrade, it's OK; if it does, it's *haram*. Nevertheless you don't need to work it all out by yourself by the light of your own reason but accept that there are principles behind Allah's commands and prohibitions, whether you immediately see the logic in them or not. The whole modern age of people sleeping with whomever they want and consuming whatever they like, is people trying to work everything out for their own benefit without considering Allah's principles.

Another principle is that anything which leads to prohibited things is also prohibited. What is doubtful should also be avoided in case it eventually involves a person in something that is unlawful. It is considered foolish to place oneself in a position where one can easily be tempted.

These laws, in Islam, are not just for adults – they are for everyone and apply equally as much to teenagers, who are really just young adults with just as much responsibility, boys and girls alike; there is no regard to sex, status, wealth or any other criterion. The most eminent head of state and the lowliest beggar are all subject to the same principles of Islam.

Islam is a way of life that you should be able to accept joyfully. It is different from the other religions of the world, many of which are remains of ancient and not-so-ancient Islams, in that it requires submission to Allah in every aspect of life, every second of the day. You must learn to subject every single detail of everything you do or think to the most careful scrutiny. The whole of life has to be taken seriously.

What about the modern world? The Qur'an was given so long ago – how can it still apply? Muslims maintain that even though life and society change, the principles and judgements taught in the Qur'an – its standards, values and injunctions – are not subject to change, no matter what the prevalent values of the society or the opinions of the majority happen to be. Personal or public opinion can never make a right wrong or a wrong right and no humans can alter a Divine law.

So, while there may be vast changes in lifestyles or ways of doing things in different societies and different eras, the principles of Islam may not be altered or in any way made conformable with people's desires. There is no need for compromise, for the Islam which was revealed to the Prophet Muhammad ﷺ is the same Islam and he is the same Prophet for this very age we live in.

Like all the good things Allah has given us, you must never take food and drink for granted. You have to accept them with thankfulness and use them wisely to keep you healthy. In general terms, you shouldn't waste food or eat things that will harm you and, as a Muslim, you have to obey certain specific rules. These things are especially important for Muslim girls to understand, as they will very likely be responsible for catering for a household before long.

- One of the Prophet's ﷺ sayings is that Muslims should not eat unless they are hungry and when they do eat they should not fill themselves. Moderation is the order of the day.

- We remember Allah and pronounce His name (*Bismillah* – In the Name of Allah) whenever we begin to eat or drink and end our meals with praise of Allah (*Alhamdulillah* – Praise belongs to Allah).

- If we are serious about looking for opportunities to serve Allah, we should consider it a blessing if guests come to share our meals. Muslims worldwide are renowned for their hospitality. They recognise that food, like everything else, belongs to Allah, so they share what they have willingly and cheerfully. Guests are free to accept their hospitality but Muslim guests too are expected to be moderate.

- Wasting food is a dreadful thing and nothing should ever be thrown away. Leftovers can always be stored and used again or there may be a chance to give something away to others, a neighbour, for example. If neither of these is possible, kind and generous people put out the leftovers for birds and wild animals who, particularly in winter, may well appreciate them.

- Muslims don't eat every food, but only that which is *halal* (permitted) and *tayyib* (wholesome and good). *Haram* (forbidden) foods are, for example, all pork products and meats from animals not slaughtered according to the way of Islam in the *halal* manner. That means that you must get your meat from a trustworthy Muslim butcher. Moreover it is of the character of Islam that you must be equally aware of the quality of the food you eat and its ingredients. Not only are some of the ingredients of processed foods actually *haram* but many of them are unhealthy, so along with many people, Muslim and non-Muslim, you find yourself more and more checking the ingredients lists of foods you buy.

The prohibition of eating pig-meat was quite clear in Allah's earlier revelations to the Children of Israel:

> **"These are the living things... which are forbidden to you ... the pig, because it parts the hoof and is cloven-footed, but does not chew the cud. It is unclean to you. Of their flesh you shall not eat, and their carcasses you shall not touch; they are unclean to you ... whoever touches them shall be unclean. Whoever touches their carcasses shall be unclean until the evening, and if you carry their carcasses you shall wash your clothes and be unclean until the evening."** (Leviticus 11:7-8, 26-28; Deuteronomy 14:8)

It is interesting to note that this ancient Judaic revelation goes much further and is much stricter than the Qur'an and the way of life of Islam. Generally this is the case. Allah has made the Divine law much, much simpler and easier for the Muslims than it was for earlier ancient peoples such as the Children of Israel. The Qur'an, however, being a reaffirmation of much of the essence of all ancient revelations reinforces this prohibition:

"O you who believe, eat of the good things of that We have provided for you, and be grateful to Allah if it is Him you worship. He has only forbidden you meat of an animal that dies of itself, and blood, and the flesh of the pig, and that over which any other name has been invoked besides that of Allah. But if anyone is compelled, without desiring and without repeating it then there is no guilt upon him." (Surah Al-Baqara 2:173 and see also Surah Al-Ma'ida 5:4; Surah Al-An'am 6:118-119, 121, 145-146; Surah An-Nahl 16:115)

You do not have to let these rules restrict your social life when it comes to mixing with your friends and neighbours – you may be invited to meals in houses or restaurants where people do not eat *halal* food, or you may not have *halal* food served at school and you will have to work out ways of dealing with these situations. It is not such a serious problem unless you reduce the teaching of Islam merely to dietary rules and go to great extremes yourself to make your own life difficult. What is *haram* is absolutely clear as we have said and one should avoid it. Otherwise there is almost always in any situation a huge amount of *halal* food available, vegetables, fruits, fish, cheese, eggs etc. Some people tell their hosts in advance what their food restrictions are: this is not such a problem, since increasingly, more and more people, apart from Muslims, are choosing their food with care. Vegetarianism for example, is not unusual at all. Others simply refuse invitations – which is impolite and a great pity because it loses all sorts of chances to spread knowledge and understanding of Islam among non-Muslims.

A nice touch would be to take a food contribution yourself – this is often greatly appreciated and of great interest, especially if it is something you have made yourself.

Another simple solution is to accept vegetarian food, a common response when travelling on aeroplanes (although a good tip is to ask for fish food which is generally superior). It used to be much more difficult to get food that was not cooked in animal fats such as lard, but with increasing concern about health and anxiety about coronary disease, most people cook with vegetable oils now. For schools and at work, packed lunches are another simple solution.

As regards alcohol and drugs – you don't need the brains of geniuses to know that these are highly dangerous substances and rarely do anyone any good. The word for any intoxicant is *khamr* and as the word (in*toxic*ant) implies, it is a poison (alcohol's chemical classification!). It was defined by the Caliph Umar ﷺ as "that which befogs the mind". (Hadith of Bukhari and Muslim)

Uthman ibn Affan ﷺ related a story that revealed alcohol to be so dangerous that it is almost the key of all harm:

> **"A man was brought and asked either to damage a copy of the Qur'an, or kill a child, or bow in worship to an idol, or drink alcohol, or sleep with a woman. He thought the least sinful thing would be to drink the cup of wine, so he drank it. Then he slept with the woman, killed the child, damaged the Qur'an, and bowed in worship to the idol."**

At the time of the Prophet ﷺ, the Arabs used to consume a great deal of alcohol. When people are used to drinking it, it is very difficult to give it up. The Qur'an gave its injunctions prohibiting alcohol step-by-step:

"From the fruit of the date-palm and the vine you derive (both) an intoxicant and a wholesome provision. Truly in that there is a sign for a people who use their intellects." (Surah An-Nahl 16:67)

"They ask you about wine and gambling. Say: 'In both of them there are great wrong and also benefits for people. And the wrong of the two of them is greater than the benefit of them.'" (Surah Al-Baqara 2:219)

"O you who believe, do not approach the prayer when you are intoxicated until you know what you are saying..." (Surah An-Nisa' 4:43)

"O you who believe, wine, and gambling, sacrificial altars of stone, and trying to foretell the future are only filth from the work of Shaytan so avoid it in order that you might succeed. Shaytan only wants to stir up among you enmity and hatred with wine and gambling, and to divert you from the remembrance of Allah and from the prayer." (Surah Al-Ma'ida 5:90-91)

As the news of this last clear command spread among the Muslims of Madinah, the effect was dramatic. Those who were drinking at the time poured away the drinks in their hands; they went through their houses and establishments smashing the wine containers, pouring the liquid out on to the sand, never to return to alcohol again. This happened some 1,400 years ago. Every committed Muslim ever since has equally totally renounced alcohol.

The problem is that you may be drawn into the company of friends who take alcohol and drugs for granted and who ridicule you for being so goody-goody or who put considerable amounts of pressure on you to try them. Alcohol is promoted as being socially acceptable by so much of the popular media. Drinks are produced at the slightest social opportunity, so much so that it is made to appear almost rude if a drink is not offered. Films and TV do four things; firstly they make alcohol appear normal and acceptable – people seem to make straight for the drinks cabinet every time they come in; secondly they encourage the mental connection between the pleasures of drinking and sex, which increases its tempting properties; thirdly they portray people who drink as being rather sophisticated and smart; and fourthly, they either show drunks as being harmless and funny or as being down-and-out, disgusting and dangerous – and you would not identify yourself with either of these last two categories.

Most people react in a negative way to the obvious drunk – but they are less clear as to where the cut-off point comes. At what stage does a person cease to be harmless and amusing and become dangerous? The Prophet Sulayman ﷾ warned that alcohol "bites like a serpent and secretes poison just like a viper". (Proverbs 23:32)

Some people drink because they think it will calm down their nerves, boost their confidence and help them both forget and face up to their problems. This is a big mistake – alcohol is a depressant and not a stimulant. The apparent uplift people feel after drinking is because alcohol depresses the anxiety level and the drinker feels less worried and more relaxed. The trouble is that alcohol has a rebound effect and after a couple of hours when the sedative effect wears off, the anxiety level bounces back – but not back to normal. It jumps to a higher level and one feels more tense and anxious than one did before. Alcohol "withdrawal" can last for up to twelve hours and when it wears off, the problems are still there.

Everyone knows how dangerous drivers are when they have been drinking. The alcohol in two cans of beer can slow a driver's reaction by two-fifths of a second, allowing a car travelling at 55mph to go an extra thirty-four feet – and a near-miss to become a crash. Alcohol creates an illusion of well-being, making the driver feel he or she is in perfect or even enhanced control, when in fact their abilities are much diminished. It is even riskier for young drivers because they are inexperienced both at drinking and driving. You should never get in a car with a driver who has been drinking or let a friend drive if he or she has been drinking. This may upset your friends but if they have any sense they will appreciate it when they come to their senses.

As Muslims you are asked not to take alcohol yourself, not to encourage others to take it, not to trade in it and not to place yourself in a situation where you can be tempted by it.

> "Allah has cursed *khamr*, those who produce it, those for whom it is produced, those who drink it, those who serve it, those who carry it, those it is carried to, those who sell it and those who buy it." (Hadith of at-Tirmidhi)

It is all too common these days to see Muslims who do drink and this weakness is a great pity. All the excuses are irrelevant to Muslims simply because Allah commanded you not to touch this substance and if you cared about His command that would really be the end of the story.

Smoking cigarettes is another unpleasant habit to definitely reject. Smoking is not actually forbidden by name in the Qur'an because the revelation came before the invention of cigarettes from tobacco. But tobacco, particularly in huge quantities of really low-grade leaf, is a harmful substance and nicotine is a drug. It is certainly against the spirit of Islam and should be regarded as something to avoid as far as possible.

Drugs are also intoxicants which are forbidden to Muslims. Marijuana, cocaine, heroin, crack, ecstasy – these have become as much a part of some teenagers' lives as rock or rap music but taking them is far from being clever – they are, to different degrees, lethal traps. Many people get drawn into the drugs scene through boredom, curiosity or as a way to escape their problems. Some do it to escape depression, others for sheer pleasure, hoping that that elusive product might exist in a chemical substance.

Emotional growth comes from facing life's problems and seeking Allah's will in them, not trying to escape them. People who use chemical props are hindering their emotional development and failing to develop the skill needed for coping with their lives and their problems.

Most of us realise that hard drugs can kill us but some seem to regard all the warnings about soft drugs as just scare tactics. Chemical substances have a vast range of psychological and biological effects, many of which are harmful to human health. There is growing evidence, for example, that smoking marijuana or cannabis can be just as likely to cause cancer as smoking tobacco and we have not even talked about the deleterious effects of tobacco. There is evidence that these substances damage the brain permanently and may bring about defects in genetic material and thus harm future children.

If you get in with the wrong crowd, you are asking for trouble. To put it bluntly, if your friends start using drugs or alcohol, you are under serious emotional pressure to conform, to fit in. CHANGE YOUR FRIENDS. If you do not change your circle of friends, you will in all likelihood start using these substances too.

You may be curious about drugs and their effects but you don't have to take them yourself or pollute your own mind and body to know what these substances do to people. You just observe the drug abusers of your own age – especially those who have been at it for a long time. Are they delightful and charming people or are they rather the misfits that people either despise or feel very sorry for?

Have a look at addicts who have grown older. Where has it got them? Frequently they are no longer "high" or seeking enjoyable experiences; they are desperate thieves, stealing even from their loved ones to finance their habits; they become beggars; their families give them up in heartbroken despair at their wasted lives. They become ill and, sooner or later, they die. There are very, very few *old* drug addicts.

If you have ever taken something that is *haram*, do not despair. Allah has also forbidden you to hate, to be spiteful, to be proud or mean, to backbite, to lie and cheat. Unless you are a saint you will probably do some or all of these at some time or another. Either you believe you cannot be forgiven your weakness and that Allah will consign you to Hell for it; or you believe that He is truly the Merciful, the Compassionate, who will accept your repentance and forgive you. The important thing is that you sincerely repent and refrain.

The Importance of Friends

Some people think there is nothing to do when choosing friends – they are simply the people we go to school with or those who live near us. A little more serious thought will show that there is all the difference between these people, whom we would call our acquaintances and the narrower selection of people we can call our friends. Making a friend involves selection and choice and often involves considerable sacrifices.

Of course, a Muslim is ready and willing to help any person who needs help but friends come into a special category. These are the ones who will stand by us when we are really low, the ones whom we would defend against all odds when they are under attack either physically or verbally.

Some friends come and go but a really good friend often lasts us for life. Friends really matter. Sometimes we make a friend within a week or so of starting at a new school and that person sticks with us until we leave several years later. If these friendships break up, it causes terrible grief and distress (which few people understand, of course).

There are few things worse in life than a friend who betrays us or turns against us or who we suddenly discover we cannot trust. We might find out someone's real feelings about us were hurtful and not at all what we expected. Nobody is perfect, not us, not them – but true friends are more valuable than pure gold and they need looking after carefully. We do not have the right to expect people to love us automatically. We have to earn that right. Before you can have friends, you have to be a friend.

Friendship plays a vital role in moulding our thinking and attitudes and it can also influence our spirituality and moral well-being and, beyond us, the well-being of society as a whole. So much depends on the wisdom with which we choose our friends.

> **"A person is on the path of his intimate friend so let each of you look carefully at whom he takes as an intimate."** (Hadith of Abu Dawud)

Friends can have a tremendous influence on us. They can make us braver (or more foolhardy, depending on how you look at these things), or kinder, or more selfish and aggressive than we would normally be. False friends can easily lead us astray and get us into trouble. We do not want to look silly in the eyes of our friends and we do not want to be left out – so if our friends are doing something wrong there is a very strong pressure on us to do it as well.

This is why Allah, in His infinite wisdom, insisted that Muslims should choose their friends with care. Help everybody, yes; care about everybody, yes; but count as our friends only a certain sort of person.

> **"O you who believe! Do not take intimate friends from outside yourselves, who will spare no pains to ruin you, and who love what harms you."** (Surah Al 'Imran 3:118)

Why should Allah be so restrictive? Isn't variety the "spice of life"? Well, maybe – but Allah knows that when we mix with people who do not trust Him as we do, there are many extra dangers and temptations that we will have to face. It is not so much the fault of our friends but of *Shaytan* – who never misses an opportunity to do something to bring people down.

The fact is that when people take anything really seriously, it almost automatically stirs up opposition. It is like throwing a stone into a pool – you cannot do it without making splashes and causing waves. Consequently, if we seriously try to live the lives of Muslims, we will find it makes waves amongst our friends and many will resent it, feel threatened by it, dislike it and, when we probably least expect (certainly on those occasions when we are feeling weak and low), will attack it. The attacks are not always open, of course – it's a brave soldier who faces the enemy head on; what they usually do is hide behind a rock and snipe.

What does Allah say? The passage about friends from among those who do not trust Allah continues:

"… who will spare no pains to ruin you, and who love what harms you. Hatred has already appeared from their mouths and that which their breasts conceal is greater. … There! You are those who love them and they don't love you and you believe in the Book, all of it (The Tawrah, the Injeel, and the Qur'an, etc.). When they meet you they say: 'We believe.' … If a good thing befalls you it troubles them. And if an evil chance befalls you they rejoice at it. And if you are patient and fearfully obedient (to Allah) their plan will not harm you."
(Surah Al 'Imran 3:118-120)

Allah did not insist that all our friends should be real Muslims, nevertheless His advice that we should prefer people of like mind to ourselves over non-believers is crystal clear:

"Let not the believers take the unbelievers as allies in preference to the believers. And whoever does that then he has nothing to do with Allah unless it be that you merely take precautions against them."
(Surah Al 'Imran 3:28)

Many young people (and old nowadays) are sadly lacking in maturity, both mental and spiritual. Many have viewpoints and opinions that are unsound, unreliable and even reckless. If a young person comes under the control of the gang, it may literally be a case of the blind leading the blind and the results can be disastrous. They edge us towards outrageous or dangerous behaviour; their influence can be very oppressive. We dread being unpopular because it can mean we will not just be ignored, but actually taunted, bullied and abused.

While it is easy to say we are not bothered by what other people think, it is quite another matter to actually stand up to the pressure of our "friends", but Muslims are warned against friendships with people who may take them from the straight path.

> **"On the day when the wrongdoer will bite upon his hands, he will say: 'O would that I had taken a path along with the Messenger, O woe is me, would that I had not taken so-and-so as an intimate friend; he certainly led me astray from the remembrance after it had come to me.'"** (Surah Al-Furqan 25:27-29)

We may be disliked and ridiculed – but who has the greater strength? Those who give in to their passion and emotions, or those who can say "No" to improper desires? Where are they headed in life, those who ridicule us? Is that where we want our lives to end up also? Is it possible that those who make our lives a misery are simply jealous of us and are covering up their own insecurity by ridicule?

Muslims are not expected to mix freely with people who take faith as a joke or belittle it. If we see evil in any situation and are able to do something about putting it right, then it is our duty to act in the best way we can. If we cannot do anything to help or improve the situation, it is better to withdraw and keep apart.

> **"Leave alone those who take their religion as play and amusement and whom the worldly life has deceived. And remind (them) of it in case a soul should be delivered to ruin because of that which it has earned..."** (Surah Al-An'am 6:70)

Islam is such a demanding way of life that it is natural that we Muslims find our support, affection and kindred feeling amongst other Muslims – regardless of national origin, language or cultural habits. We provide each other with encouragement for living in Islam and act as deterrent for deviating from it.

> **"And the believing men and the believing women are protecting friends to one another. They command what is right and forbid what is wrong and they establish the salat and produce the zakat and they obey Allah and His Messenger."** (Surah Al-Tawba 9:71)

Friends should stick together and care for each other. We cannot call ourselves real friends if we do not pay attention when our friends are suffering.

> "You see the believers in their mutual love, affection and mercy like one body; when one member has a complaint the rest of the body is united with it in wakefulness and fever." (Hadith of Bukhari)

> "Believers are to one another like a building whose parts support one another." (Hadith of Bukhari)

> "By Him in Whose hand is my soul, none you believes until he loves for his brother what he loves for himself." (Hadith of Bukhari)

Remember that although these ahadith speak of "he" they really mean "he" and "she", both male and female. The duties are the same for every person regardless of sex. Caring for our friends brings great rewards, both in this life and in the next:

> "A Muslim is a Muslim's brother; he does not wrong him or abandon him. If anyone cares for his brother's need, Allah will care for his need; if anyone removes his brother's anxiety, Allah will remove from him one of the anxieties on the Day of Resurrection; and if anyone conceals a Muslim's secrets, Allah will conceal his secrets on the Day of Resurrection." (Hadith of Bukhari and Muslim)

What happens if we haven't got any friends? Loneliness is a warning signal. Hunger warns us that we need food, loneliness warns us that we need companionship. You need companionship to feel valued, to feel well. If we are chronically lonely, we need to try to understand the cause.

Sometimes it comes from within – we have low self-esteem and cannot believe that anyone could like us, let alone love us. The key here is to build up our self-respect. Get involved with other people, widen out. Caring for other people takes our minds off our own loneliness and motivates others to take an interest in us. Start with a smile. Don't wait for others to speak – speak first. Do kind acts and show a generous spirit. Relax. Set realistic goals and make Allah our closest friend.

Maybe we cannot make friends because we are shy? Shyness is extreme self-consciousness, feeling awkward around people – strangers, those in authority, the opposite sex and so on. Some become embarrassed and find they can't speak; others chatter continuously and irritate others. Shyness is not really a bad thing, it is akin to modesty and humility; it is good to be discreet. It is only harmful when it negatively affects our relationships, work and feelings.

Remember that shyness doesn't describe what we are, only our behaviour and how we react to situations. We may think others are making negative judgements about us or that they don't like us or that they are better or more "normal" than us. We are extremely sensitive to other people's opinions and often we are too sensitive. We tense up because we have formed certain conclusions – but the good news is that it is not at all likely that they are true.

If you keep withdrawing you may give the wrong impression, that you are stuck-up, unfriendly, bored, uncaring or ignorant. Your thoughts are on yourself, so you are not paying attention to what is being discussed. Then, if you don't pay enough attention to the information you are receiving, what you most fear happens – you look stupid.

Shyness can be a part of *Iman*. It comes from your high opinion of the value of others. But there is a shyness that is your high opinion of your own worth and the thought that no-one else will know your value. Which do you have? You must stop worrying about whether or not the other person is evaluating you. Try to think positively. Everybody has strengths and weaknesses, likes and dislikes. Just because somebody does not agree with you does not mean that they have rejected you as a person – just that they don't agree with you. Try to develop some interest, or be skilful and competent in something, so that you do not feel so insecure yourself.

We have to stick by our true friends. A false friend will stab us in the back – a true friend will stick up for us. Don't expect perfection – we all make mistakes. The cost of friendship is nothing compared to the cost of not loving – a life of empty loneliness.

Let us think about our manners and our way of dealing with people. The Prophet ﷺ was a living example of the finest and most beautiful manners and he stressed politeness and consideration as expressions of a Muslim's faith. Basically, this means to treat others as they wish to be treated and as we like to be treated ourselves, whether they are Muslims or non-Muslims, relatives, friends, strangers or even enemies.

It seems obvious that we are generally drawn to friends who think much in the same way as we do – and, as we have seen, Allah encourages us to choose our friends in this way. However, we should not let this result in a kind of off-putting exclusiveness, which does nothing for *da'wah* (calling people to Allah).

Visiting friends and being concerned for them is important. There is no prescribed number of times we should visit in a week, but it should be often enough that a friend does not feel neglected. Whenever we meet a friend, we should be concerned about his or her family and their welfare. If there is any difficulty there, ask them is there any way that I could help? Sometimes going to the shops for someone is an enormous help and not much trouble to us. Don't wait for your friend to visit you before you go to him or her. Treat your friend's parents as you would your own and show great respect to them.

If your friends are also your neighbours, there are special considerations to bear in mind. The most important thing is not to behave in any way that would upset or harm them – such as raising our voices, shouting or having loud noisy music or parties at night, or doing anything in our gardens (within their view) which would upset or offend them.

Do things for them and send them little gifts from time to time. Invite them to dinner, or if your mother has made too many cakes, ask if she will send a few to them.

If you fall out with your friend next door, it is your duty as a Muslim not to let your conflict interfere with the relationship your parents and their parents enjoy.

Muslims offer help before it is asked for, if we see that it is needed. Also, if we overhear anything private, we should keep it to ourselves.

If you are invited to a meal or a party, it is polite to accept, otherwise the friend might feel hurt and snubbed. When going to a meal in somebody's house, you do not have the right to bring along anybody else, without the host's permission. If you are invited by someone you know is not good company for you, you might accept if there is any possibility that your company may be good for them and your influence may start to bring them back to the right way. Don't lose any opportunity for *da'wah* – and this is not "preachifying", but showing the standard of your conduct and kindness. Remember that this does more for the image of Islam than the articulation of the mouth.

If you intend to visit someone, it is good manners to tell them first and give them an opportunity to refuse you if it is not convenient for them and you should not feel offended by this (you may yourself have to refuse someone's intended visit). If you have made an arrangement, you should keep to the times promptly and if something crops up to prevent you from going, you should certainly let your host know.

You should not enter another's home until you have permission and try to remember at all times that you are in someone else's home and fit in with it. It is impolite to refuse what you are offered, even if you don't particularly like it, unless it is *haram* food or drink, or there is a medical reason or you are fasting. In these cases, you should apologise and make sure your host knows before you start.

Don't be offensive in body odours when in company – watch out for clothes, body and mouth; not too much scent or garlic.

As Muslims we try not to make ourselves nuisances by staying too long and wearing out our welcome. We thank our hosts for what they have done for us and ask permission before we leave.

> **"The one who does not thank creatures does not thank the Creator."** (Hadith of Abu Dawud)

A simple way to thank is to say, *"Jazakallah khayran"* – "May Allah reward you well."

Muslims should listen politely when people are talking to them and not interrupt others when they are speaking. They face the person who is speaking and show interest and meet their eye from time to time. They try to avoid pointless arguments with those who disagree with them.

The key quality in a good friendship is unselfishness, thinking about others before yourself. If you can remember to put others first, this will lead almost automatically to the spreading of affection and goodwill and the forging of life-long friendships.

Coping
with the Family

> "O Allah, make my love for You greater than any other love, my fear of You greater than any other fear. Make my eagerness to meet You cut across all my worldly desires. Give the worldly their pleasure in this world, but let my pleasure be in worshipping You."
> (Hadith of at-Tirmidhi and al-Hakim)

If we are blessed in this world, we are born into a caring devout family and grow up surrounded by people who deeply love us. If we are blessed, we have parents we respect, grandparents we treasure for their kindness and wisdom, brothers and sisters who support and comfort us. Later we hope to have husbands and wives who will love and cherish us and who will build successful homes with us and by whom we will in our turn produce our own children, who will also love us, insha'Allah.

That's the theory. Some of us know that in practice it does not always work out as simply as that. Allah certainly knows it and drops several hints in the Qur'an to warn us not to be too unrealistic in our hopes for that blissful, untroubled family life.

"Know that your possessions and your children are but a trial and that Allah, with Him there is a vast reward."
(Surah Al-Anfal 8:28)

Many human beings are selfish, greedy, weak, insecure, demanding and so on. It is pointless pretending that sometimes the people in our own families are not like that and pointless to deny that we sometimes have a problem coping with them. Sometimes, of course, the problems are all of our own making – it is *we* who have the chip on our shoulders, or whose character is lazy or lacking in some way and, therefore, all the hassle from our parents is really our fault and is deserved.

Nevertheless, sometimes it is *not* our fault and things don't work out in the family as intended.

Even so, it is quite ordinary for people to consider that the claim of the family on their hearts and minds, on their attention and loyalty, or on their time and wealth, is prior to any other claim. In any relationships, they feel it is right that the family should come first. Blood is thicker than water, as they say. Even when they become adults and strive to acquire worldly possessions and wealth, it is usually not just for selfish reasons, but because they love and are responsible for others – their families.

Islam makes it crystal clear that the well-being of the family is important to Allah; it is an organic unit which He has created and blessed, for the wellbeing of every individual and for society as a whole.

> **"He is the One who created you from one self and created from it its spouse that he might dwell with her."** (Surah Al-A'raf 7:189)

> **"And Allah made for you of your houses a dwelling."** (Surah An-Nahl 16:80)

Yet, Allah also makes it clear that when we commit ourselves to Him, our relationship with Him must take precedence over everything else, even our families. Sometimes, we are called to be Muslims *in spite of* our families.

When we make a commitment to Allah that we will try our utmost to serve and love Him and do His will as far as we can in this life, then we may one day have to make decisions that place our service to Allah above the wishes of our family.

"And We have counselled man with good treatment of his parents. And if they strive with you to make you associate as partners with Me that of which you have no knowledge then do not obey them." (Surah Al-Ankabut 29:8)

This certainly happened to the Prophet Ibrahim ﷺ when he had to go against the traditions of his parents who were idol-worshippers and later on in his life, when he was asked to sacrifice his own dearly-loved son as a test of his obedience.

"And Ibrahim's seeking forgiveness for his father was only because of a promise he had made him. Then when it became clear to him that he was an enemy of Allah he disassociated himself from him. Truly Ibrahim was compassionate and forbearing." (Surah Al-Tawba 9:114)

Similarly, Prophet Nuh ﷺ was called on to disassociate himself from his son.

"And Nuh called upon his Lord and said, 'O my Lord, truly my son is from my family and surely Your promise is the truth and You are the Most Just of Judges'. He said, 'O Nuh, truly he was not of your family. He was a (person of) unrighteous action. So do not ask Me of that of which you have no knowledge.'" (Surah Hud 11:45-46)

We always hope that we will not be forced to go against our parents, but it can sometimes happen when our deepest principles are involved. We are only human and our parents are only human too. This means that everyone is capable of making mistakes. If our parents are trying to force or tempt us away from what is the correct way of serving Allah, then we have to find the courage to say, "Sorry – this I cannot do."

This is important, because ultimately, when we stand before Allah on Judgement Day, our family relationships will no longer be taken into consideration.

> **"You will not find a people who believe in Allah and the Last Day loving whoever opposed Allah and His Messenger even if they were their parents or their children or their brethren or their relatives."**
> (Surah Al-Mujadala 58:22)

Our Prophet ﷺ taught that when we are living with parents or other family members who do not perhaps share our thoughts and beliefs, we do not have the right to try and force our beliefs on them – **"Let there be no compulsion into the religion"** (Surah Al-Baqara 2:256) – just as they do not have the right to force their beliefs upon us. If we are convinced that we are in the right and they are wrong, then we should be firm in our beliefs, but gentle and considerate with them. Islam teaches respect for the beliefs of others, while at the same time hoping that they will be drawn towards Islam.

"I do not worship what you worship, and you will not worship that which I worship … To you your way and to me mine."
(Surah Al-Kafirun 109:2-3, 6)

"And if they (your parents) strive with you to make you associate as partners with Me that of which you have no knowledge then do not obey them. And keep company with them in this world in a good manner."
(Surah Luqman 31:15)

It is a terribly difficult task if we have to live with people who disagree with us or actually dislike our ways. For a start, we are expected to love and honour our parents and indeed, it is right to do so. But as we become adults, we have to realise that our duty to Allah and our love of Him comes before our love of them. If they want us to do something contrary to the command of Allah (or prevent us from doing something that Allah has commanded) – which, please God, they will not – then we are obliged to set aside our obedience of them and this is hardly an easy matter.

"And when it is said to them, 'Follow that which Allah has revealed', they said: 'Rather, you will follow that which you found your parents (and forefathers) doing'. What, even if their parents (and forefathers) did not reason at all and were not guided?"
(Surah Al-Baqara 2:170)

If things seem hopeless, remember always that you do not remain a teenager forever and as an adult, you have far more control over the circumstances of your life. While you are so dependent on your parents for your home, food and clothing, it is only right to respect them, be polite to them and try not to hurt their feelings. Control of the tongue is such a difficult thing, but often called for. You must remember that Allah sees everything, the innermost thoughts of your heart, your struggle, your honest attempts to do the right thing, even if everyone thinks you are wrong, or even if you are wrong. Allah, praise be to Him, always sees your intention and your motivation and knows all the circumstances in a way deeper than you even do yourself.

When we are involved in trouble and conflict, it is all too easy to get bogged down in it and not be able to take a wider view. That is why talking to others, especially people who have gone through the same kind of thing as us, can be a wonderful help and eye-opener.

It is Allah's will for parents to have authority within the family and we have to recognise their God-given right to make rules for us. It is true that other parents may be more lenient than ours are, but our parents have the task of deciding what is best for us, until they are convinced that we can do this for ourselves. (Even then, they may continue to give us advice until their last breath, because they love us always).

Honouring your parents means accepting correction without sulking or throwing tantrums or cutting them out of your life. You must not regard them as idiots but as the most precious of beings. They are the ones who love us the most – even if they are sometimes arbitrary, unfair, hot-tempered or even downright wrongdoing. Should you honour any person who is not worthy of honour? Yes – because although our parents are less than perfect, they have also made many sacrifices for us, which we probably do not realise.

Just because a parent's example is not the best in the world, it does not mean that everything they tell us is wrong. Sometimes, as we grow in wisdom, we see that we have to "do as they tell us" and not act as they do.

What if the parent is seriously wrong? Stay calm. Rebellion accomplishes nothing, neither does hateful, spiteful behaviour. We have to be on our guard that our behaviour does not become hurtful. Parents are answerable to Allah for the things they say and do and we are answerable for the things we say and do. On That Day, no one makes excuses or allowances for anybody else, not even for the next of kin.

Sometimes it is better to forgive and forget a parent's hurtful actions and focus on their good qualities rather than dwell on their faults. It is possible, for example, that your father or mother cannot show demonstrative love to you because he or she grew up in an unloving and overrestrained atmosphere and was never taught how to show affection. You may never know what hurts and traumas they endured; they may have chosen to protect you from that knowledge. Thoughtless words may stab them and cause pain but they will not solve your problems.

Often young people wear themselves (and their parents) out resisting parental instructions only to find out later that their parents were right all along.

Suppose we do want to respect our parents but feel misunderstood and hemmed in by restrictions, how could we improve our situation? If our parents are critical of, or not interested in, the things we think important, this can be very frustrating. Before we can expect our parents to understand us, we must understand them, because before we can expect anyone at all to understand us, we must have endeavoured to understand them.

Recognising that our parents are simply humans with feelings like ours is a big first step. If they are not as idealistic as us, it may be because difficult personal experience has given them wisdom born of real experience. They may actually feel quite insecure about their ability to rear us properly. They may feel overwhelmed by the moral dangers and temptations that they know we will have to face. They may overreact.

They may also be struggling with physical, financial or emotional hardships that we do not fully understand. A father may dislike his job and be patiently trying to find ways to change it but never complain; he will hardly be sympathetic to us when we complain that we hate school.

Communication is the key to improvement of relationships. If some conflict arises, you should first ask yourself whether your parent was not feeling well or was worried over something else. Were they hurt by some thoughtless word or deed on your part and therefore not feeling very obliging towards you? Did they perhaps just misunderstand what you meant?

Genuinely getting through to the other party is important. We must choose a good time to talk, not when they are busy or upset or involved in something else. If they seem too busy to care, say something assertive like – "I know you're busy, but something is really troubling me. Can we talk?" Don't forget to use words parents will understand – the street jargon of pals could be quite meaningless to them or have some other meaning.

If you are about to confess some awful thing you have done, your parents may well feel hurt and disappointed, so you shouldn't be surprised or indignant if they lash out with heated words. If you had listened to their warnings earlier, you probably wouldn't be in the situation you are in. So stay calm, be humble, don't water down the truth and don't try to hold back the less pleasant details. Be prepared to accept some discipline, if it is deserved.

Remember, this will almost certainly not be the last time you will need your parents' help and mature advice. If you get into the habit of confiding in them over the small things, then when the big things come along you won't find it so difficult to tell them what is on your mind. Even the most saintly of parents has skeletons in the cupboard, things they have done that they are probably ashamed to talk about.

Try to tell them how you feel – speaking straight from the heart can help to settle so many misunderstandings. This does not mean, of course, that your parents will immediately swing round to your point of view. No such luck! Many times, parents are still going to say no. This does not mean that they do not understand you, just that they disagree with you and wish to forestall disaster. Sulking, lying or openly being disobedient will not encourage parents to treat you as an adult. Don't make childish demands or whine. If you want more freedom and responsibility, you must prove yourself responsible. Remember "responsible" means to be "liable to be called to account".

How can you do that? Well, for a start you can take seriously the things your parents want you to do. Use your own initiative. You don't need a specific command from your parents when there are obvious things that need doing – dishes to be washed up, shopping or ironing to be done, rooms to be cleared up, little ones to be looked after. Nothing pleases a parent more than finding they have offspring who can see what needs doing and don't need to be asked to help.

If you have persuaded your parents to let you have a part-time job, prove that you can organise and save some money and not just waste it. Prove to them that you do not just want to spend your pocket-money on things they probably disapprove of like violent DVDs, sexually explicit pop music, make-up or expensive flashy clothing. If you are earning a reasonable sum, have you volunteered to make some contribution to the household? If your family actually observe your adult manner of handling your time and money, they will be much more inclined to grant you the freedoms you desire and to trust you.

Use your abilities to make decisions for yourself. Don't go running to your parents at the first sign of distress. Start practising the ability to stand on your own two feet – then, when you need to, you will be much more able to cope. Don't keep running to your mother and father asking what to do – think the situation through, work out what seems the best thing to you to do and then explain it to them and see what their observations are. Once they see that you are no longer thinking and acting as a child, you will have become an adult.

If your parents are particularly strict and do not like you going out at all after school, try to show them that you have no intention of behaving in an immodest or loud and vulgar manner. They are worried that you may be influenced by the wrong sort of company – so it would help if you could bring your friends home and introduce them to your parents, let them see what sort of people they are. If your parents really do not approve of your friends, try to consider why this is. Take a long, cool look at them. Most parents are not really so unreasonable.

You may tell your parents that all your friends go out and do this or that, but your parents will not regard their lives as any of your business. They will want you to behave with patience and restraint and if they are really Muslims and you are a girl, they will probably take the point of view that the Prophet ﷺ would have disapproved of girls above the age of puberty hanging out on the streets for no good and useful purpose. He knew then, as your parents know now, that life on the streets leads to all sorts of problems. Your parents will not wish you to start wanting to go to clubs or pubs, which is what they know a lot of your friends will soon want to do. Apart from anything else, they know this leads to sexual temptation (which leads to unwanted babies, single parents etc.) and they wish to keep you safe from this.

It is partly that they fear you will be seduced and give in to the very powerful emotional and sexual urges which are particularly strong in all healthy young adult animals, whatever the species. Then, there is also the fear of dangerous and predatory men who commit rape and mentally sick men who might seize any chance to take advantage of unwary women and children.

For some strange reason, some men seem to think rape is something that can be laughed at and not very serious. You even hear some wise-guys sniggering about women raping men – which is complete nonsense. Women can seduce men (something they might enjoy) but they cannot *rape* them. Probably the revolting fact that many predatory men now prefer to rape little boys or young men rather than girls, in a form of sexual activity totally forbidden by the Prophet

ﷺ, will bring back the feeling of shock and outrage and hurt that this crime causes. Always remember that rapists do not choose their victims because they are pretty or sexually attractive – but because they are vulnerable and unprotected. The news is full of men who have attacked even aged grandmothers.

Nowadays, you must be very careful about which sites you visit on the internet and remember never ever to give out your details to anyone or to chat with someone you do not know.

Bear in mind that your parents are probably much more aware of these dangers than you are – so don't be offended if they seem "over-the-top" in wanting to know where you are and who you are with and how you will get home.

Above all, do not become deceitful or shifty, trying to get away with things behind parents' backs. This is never a good idea and you feel such fools anyway if you are caught out, as you almost inevitably will. Try the Muslim way, suggested in the Qur'an to put things right between husbands and wives when they have differences – they have to discuss things through with the help of another person on each side.

> **"If you fear a breach between the two of them, appoint two arbiters, one from his family and the other from hers; if they wish reconciliation Allah will make harmony and agreement between them."**
> (Surah An-Nisa' 4:35)

This is something you could try in your situation. Your parents will respect you far more once they understand that they can trust you and once they are convinced that you always tell them the truth.

If you are a Muslim, you will be truthful and trustworthy. Why? Because the truth is important – Allah is The Truth, The Real and because being a believer is to begin to trust Him, whose consequence will be that you are trustworthy in turn. If what you want to do, against your parents' wishes, is something that you are slightly ashamed of discussing openly with them – then your own conscience is telling you something and the chances are that they are right and you are wrong and you should think again about whatever it is you want to do.

But what happens if things get really bad? Perhaps it is not just the old culture rubbing up against the new, but that your family have actively turned against Islam, or have never been Muslims. Suppose they simply refuse to believe in what you believe? Or suppose they are openly hostile to Islam? They make fun of you or treat you with contempt. They may even, if it comes to it, drive you away or disown you.

This is always a very hurtful situation. We have to take comfort from the knowledge that no slave of Allah escapes this sort of problem – if the Prophet Muhammad ﷺ had to go through so much with his own family, especially his uncles, we should not imagine that we will get away without being tested in this way.

We should look upon our relationships with our families as all part and parcel of our test of life. If we think like this, we will realise that we are not alone, not at all, but Allah is with us, observing our struggle, caring for our hurt, pleased when we stand firm in spite of everything, delighted when we can acquire the grace to do everything for Him and still maintain happy dignified relationships with our families despite the differences.

Sex, Honour
and Modesty

The bottom line is that Allah has refused permission for any sexual activity outside marriage.

This means that all Muslims (young and old) either marry or control themselves and do not encourage the kind of behaviour that leads to temptation and immorality. Men should behave respectfully towards women – no matter how tempting or helpless they happen to be. Women should behave modestly and not in such a way as to inflame a man's desires or make him yearn after what he should not have. Even if we think we have fallen in love, it is our business as Muslims to remember Allah and control our urges and not do anything that would displease Allah or make us and our family ashamed.

There are lots of advantages in being a Muslim, although we may think our parents very strict while we are young. For example, a Muslim woman claims the right to be a protected virgin before her marriage, a beloved wife, a respected mother and a cherished grandmother – and also expects Muslim society not to leave her against her inclination to live alone or without protection, help or a natural sexual relationship. Therefore Muslim men have the duty and responsibility not to cut themselves off from women or live celibate lives (without sexual relationships), but to make themselves the best marriage-partners they can possibly be.

That is part of the contract. If you and your life-partner are not going to indulge in sexual relationships outside of your marriage, then it is the pleasant duty of both of you to make sure that you are both happy and content with the intimate side of your marriage.

It seems that the permissive society of the West has become so tolerant of sex outside marriage, illegitimacy, exploitation and greed as to be actually guilty of encouraging these things. Unwise "freedom" has contributed strongly to the psychological and emotional stress in society and has particularly damaged the family unit – as you yourself may know if you or any of your friends come from broken homes. In the average classroom, over a third of the students will not be living with their own fathers and mothers! It is worth remembering that when you take note of their insecure and attention-seeking behaviour.

Muslims are appalled by the influence of Western television – the blatant advertising of alcohol, the portrayal of sex (both normal and perverted), the acceptance of so many things they regard as socially evil. There is no check on materialism, selfishness or greed. The young seem to be condoned when they live dangerously or selfishly and the old are abandoned to end their days with strangers.

Muslims, men and women, try to live good lives and expect to be treated with respect. Allah has granted young women the right to special consideration and protection because of their physical biology. Men do not have to put up with menstruation and later pregnancy, childbirth and suckling children. Men are not usually harassed because of their attractiveness or forced to accept sex in order to get on or not lose a job.

Muslim women are no more or less beautiful than other women but they do not flaunt their attractions. Allah and His Messenger ﷺ require them to dress modestly, in such a way as not to encourage male attention and draw it towards their physical charms. Passions, if not kept under control, cause endless hurt and disturbance and, therefore, if a woman deliberately behaves in such a way as to cause temptation to men, people will think badly of her. Allah would like her to protect her charm, her beauty and her sexuality for the partner whom she will marry. Nobody thinks well of men or women who go around trying to inflame and seduce others.

In trying to maintain chastity before marriage, certain guidelines are sensible. Everyone knows how strong the sexual urges are, for some women as much as for men. Firstly, if you mix freely with people, it should never be alone with a member of the opposite sex, but in the company of a third party whose presence protects you from temptation. You may not realise the serious dangers you could face, but women need protection from sexual harassment, and handsome men from seduction. (Since harassment is highly unpleasant, whereas seduction might be highly enjoyable, it is quite probable that men will have far more desire to be left on their own with women than vice versa and will therefore need to develop strong determination and self-control).

In these days of students attending mixed schools and colleges, then going out to work in mixed society, it is not always possible for a *mahram* (a male relative who is unable to marry a woman) to be present. It is, however, usually possible to have another person around or at least for a woman not to be left alone with men. Thousands of women know, to their cost, what often happens when they are left alone with another man, be he boss, colleague, friend or even doctor. Horrifyingly, some women are not even safe from their own male relatives.

Sexual liberty and licence harm individuals, parents, unwanted children and the security of other families. Devout and loving young Muslims should not wish to seek sexual attention – and we will probably find that our parents try not to leave us free to mix with the opposite sex once we arrive at the teenage years. Many Muslim parents try to place their sons and daughters in single sex schools but this is not always possible and does not always have the desired effect anyway.

Those who observe at first hand the behaviour and talk of many of the pupils in single-sex schools, know that the talk amongst "the lads" (and often "the girls" too) can be crude and offensive. There is a kind of bravado that makes some young people compete in being vulgar and abusive. Sometimes it is deliberate, at other times it is the result of ignorance. The best way to deal with this is to behave with dignity; do not let others see that it might upset you, for some may find this an encouragement to torment you. You can simply remove yourself from the situation by walking away or by making sure that you have chosen your friends carefully in the first place. Never encourage crudity by smiling and appearing to tolerate it – but neither become aggressive and thus risk antagonism and embarrassment.

Chastity seems a very old-fashioned virtue these days, when people give the impression that everyone has indulged in sex before marriage. A lot of the talk is nothing but talk and there are still plenty of non-Muslim young people, men and women, who guard their virginity as if it was more precious than gold. Contrary to classroom opinion, there is nothing wrong or unusual in being a virgin; it makes one a special person for one's future partner.

Everyone knows the dangers of premarital sex – for the girl abortions, and for both the girl and boy premature "shot-gun" marriages, diseases and the killer AIDS. On top of that there is the psychological damage and disappointment and the shame at one's lack of self-control and diminished self-respect. Premarital sex can make people feel sick, cheap and dirty. It usually isn't all that enjoyable either. Married couples could tell you that they spend a long time sorting out their sexual relationship with each other and in marriage this can be done in an atmosphere of genuine love and commitment. Youngsters making love furtively and sporadically are not really laying down a good foundation for their future sex lives – all they are learning is self-gratification and exploitation of the other.

When you think about it, sex before marriage only breeds jealousy and distrust: "If he or she had sex with me, then probably he or she did with somebody else before me and very likely he or she will move on to yet another partner tomorrow." Young girls suffer terrible agonies when considering giving in to a young man's advances – "Will he still love me? Will he still feel the same about me tomorrow?" The answer? "Of course he won't." He may have been carried away by the strength of his feelings enough to tell her that he will love her for ever and so on, but the sad fact is that there is a perverse streak in men which makes them react quite differently to the girls who "will" and the girls who "won't".

Virginity is a very valuable gift. The person you marry is really entitled to the knowledge that you have not enjoyed anybody else. The singular fact of virginity, of course, is that once you have given it, it cannot be restored again, no matter how much you might regret what you have done. Do not lose it lightly.

There is another danger, too. Research shows that those who engage in sex before marriage are twice as likely to commit adultery afterwards. Once you have adopted the attitude that "it doesn't matter", the mere signing of a piece of paper and a marriage ceremony will not suddenly change that attitude. Anybody can be dissatisfied with their sexual partner; sexual expertise is not automatic and doesn't happen overnight. You have to make a conscious decision whether you love that person and, if you do, you have to work at the relationship, not just change partners every so often.

In marriage, a healthy, intimate sexual relationship demands restraint and self-control; the emphasis should be on giving and gratifying the other rather than on taking and self-gratification. Self-control teaches you to put unselfish concern for the other's welfare ahead of your own desires – and this is a good attitude to bring to a marriage. It is a great joy to welcome your partner and know that he or she cares for you over their self and you for him or her. Nothing can replace the confidence that this feeling of mutual care brings.

So, how can you resist those sexual urges?
- Firstly, by taking care over the things you read and view. Try to avoid stuff that will stir up the passions. A lot of magazines, films, TV programmes and so on are deliberately designed to turn people on and make them feel aroused. This is rather dangerous if you are trying to cool down your natural urges.

- Choose friends carefully; avoid people who talk loosely and disrespectfully about sex.
- Take seriously parents' desire for you not to have intimate relationships with the opposite sex, even though it may make you feel left out. Islam recommends that men and women who are not married to each other should not be left alone together because of the inevitable temptations and strains. Older people know how strong the natural forces are and they are much stronger for the young – so it is foolish to start the habit of seeking to be alone with particular friends. Retain shyness – it will do no harm.

There is nothing wrong with feeling sexual arousal. Sometimes unexpected things like tensions, fears and frustrations can cause sexual arousal and erotic dreams. If you have experienced this, there is nothing wrong with you and you have not done wrong. It is a normal response of the human body which decreases gradually with age.

Curiosity, novelty and pleasure often lead young people to arouse their own sexual organs and quite often this becomes a habit. It will not make you go blind or bald but it does tend to magnify desires that would be better calmed down. Self-arousal is often accompanied by fantasies, which are but a short step from immoral living and also lead to attitudes that are corrupting. Fantasies are never realistic, so real sex can seem disappointing and tame in comparison. Many people have very unrealistic expectations, brought about by reading erotic and pornographic literature which gives a totally wrong and distorted impression. Women also imbibe fantasies from romantic novels and comics. The heroes of these novels are as unlike real men as the sexy uninhibited sirens of "girlie" magazines are unlike real women.

During self-arousal, a person is immersed in his or her own bodily sensations – sex becomes totally self-centred and completely separated from love. There is a danger that people will come to think of men or women as sex objects to gratify their appetites and this has ruined many marriages.

Don't despair. Self-arousal is not an unforgivable sin but it is a habit as hard to kick as alcohol or smoking. The scholars of Islam would say that it is something to be disapproved of but tolerated if there is a danger of adultery or worse.

When you do meet someone that you would like to take seriously, remember that marriage is not a game. Allah intended husbands and wives to forge a strong and permanent bond, which is one of the closest relationships humans can know. It is no good marrying because of some kind of romantic illusion or to get away from home. You might have difficulties at home, but marriage presents a whole new set of matters to negotiate. Marriage is not exactly a "ball and chain", but it curbs a lot of prized liberties and gives added responsibilities.

Satisfactory sex lives grow out of unselfishness and self control, qualities many people fail to cultivate, particularly in their youth. Many husbands imagine that they can carry on living like single men without making a full commitment to their wives. Many young husbands would rather go out with their mates, play football, snooker or go to a club than do things around the house or spend time with their wives. Many young wives would rather watch TV, go out or sleep, than look after the baby, clean the house or prepare meals. They have no idea, when they marry, how this society has made the day-to-day grind so boring, nor have they learnt to cope with budgeting household expenses or to deal with those times when they don't have enough money. Some young wives expect to buy straight away many of the items that had probably taken their parents years to acquire. With little or no patience, they plunge into debt, usually with heavy interest payments which means that the debts grow bigger and bigger, day by day. It is not an accident that interest is *haram* in the *shari'ah*.

Romantic love does not conquer all or last forever, despite what films, TV and romantic novels would have you believe. Physical attraction usually only touches the outer shell, not the secret person inside. Outward appearances can be very deceiving. It is a great mistake to fall in love with a person's looks (even with a person's clothes and sense of style) and ignore what the person is inside.

> **"Do not marry for the sake of good looks alone; those looks may become the cause of moral decline. Do not marry for the sake of wealth, for this may become the cause of disobedience. Marry rather on the grounds of religious devotion."** (Hadith of at-Tirmidhi)

True love is an unselfish caring about the interests of the other, seeing their faults, yet loving them anyway. Infatuation is unrealistic and self-centred, no matter how fantastic (it is just that – a fantasy). True love has a strong basis in respect; it is not desperately craving a person's outward appearance and trying to mould him or her into a pattern that you happen to desire. True love is not hurt by time; often the best way to test love is to let time pass.

If parents want to have an arranged marriage, don't panic. If you agree to it, you have the right to come to know the intended bride or bridegroom beforehand so that you can work out for yourself some idea of his or her qualities. If your parents are trying to force or trick you into marriage, this is totally against Islam and you should seek help from your imam or another trusted person. The Prophet ﷺ did not himself set a pattern of hurrying into or hurrying others into marriages with partners who had not even been seen. He had certainly seen all his wives before marriage and some of them he had known for years.

Don't expect perfection in any person, because there is no such thing. Everybody will have some fault or other that one wishes they had not got, but then again, so do you. If you waited to find a perfect person, you would never marry at all. Marriage is a mutual caring and a sharing of life, in which you can talk about everything and find out how to make your partners happy, secure and content. This cannot be achieved overnight – it takes time and skill.

The Prophet ﷺ knew that a good marriage was one of the most important things a Muslim could gain for themselves, short of Paradise – it is half of the *deen*, a half of the life transaction, of Islam. He ﷺ said this about wives:

> **"...Should I not tell you of the best thing a man can treasure: a good woman who when he looks at him pleases him and if he tells her to do something she obeys him and if he is away from her she safeguards him."**
> (Hadith of Abu Dawud)

Half the Muslims are Women

We have throughout the book addressed the problems that young men and young women encounter in common at this age. We also need to say a few things particularly about the situation of women in general within Islam and within the Muslim world community as it is (not necessarily the same thing).

Well, of course, you all know women are inferior to men! This was apparently the view of the Arab men who lived before the time of the Prophet ﷺ. They simply regarded women as part of their property. That can still be true today of numerous men all round the world. But this attitude towards half of humanity is not what Allah revealed as His will. One day, Umm Salamah ﷺ, the wife of the Prophet ﷺ, asked him why the Qur'an did not specifically speak about women as it did about men. Later, to her surprise, she was combing her hair one afternoon, when she heard her husband's voice ringing out from the *mimbar*. The words were:

"Truly Muslim men and Muslim women, and believing men and believing women, and obedient men and obedient women, and truthful men and truthful women, and patient men and patient women, and humble men and humble women, and men who give charity and women who give charity, and men who fast and women who fast, and men who guard their private parts and women who guard, and men who remember Allah much and women who remember, Allah has prepared for them forgiveness and a vast reward. It is not for a believing man or a believing woman when Allah and His Messenger have decided a matter that they should have any choice in their affair. Whoever disobeys Allah and His Messenger has certainly gone clearly astray." (Surah Al-Ahzab 33:35-36)

The words of the Qur'an do not go on to specify man and woman (or boys and girls) every single time after this; not for one moment is this necessary. Allah, in this *ayah*, underlines what an understanding of Arabic would reveal, that plurals, such as "O you who believe", and even "they" and "you", implicitly refer to and address any number of men and women. Allah makes it perfectly clear that the service and worship of both sexes, their responsibilities and values are regarded by Him as the same.

"Their Lord answered them that, 'I do not cause the work of any of you who work, male or female, to be lost.'" (Surah Al 'Imran 3:195)

"And whoever does right action, male or female, and is a believer, then those will enter the Garden and they will not be wronged so much as the groove in a date stone." (Surah An-Nisa' 4:124)

It is not a person's gender (or age) that determines who earns the grace of Allah – it is their faith and the desire to serve and obey, from either man or woman.

No two people are equal in the sight of Allah, but we are all unique and each finds His mercy in ways which are unique to him or her. Similarly with responsibilities and duties, yet the legal duties of the *shari'ah* are very similar for men and women and very fair. Men and women, each in their own way, have as much opportunity to remember, worship and serve Allah as each other, as much chance of success or failure in the life to come. The Speech of Allah, the Qur'an, in stressing this, has been incredibly revolutionary and is still so today in this society and in so-called Muslim societies.

"Allah chooses for Himself whomever He wishes, and guides to Himself whomever (e.g. male or female) turns in penitence to Him." (Surah Ash-Shura 42:13)

"Every human, We have fastened his decree to his neck, and We will bring out for him on the Day of Resurrection a book which he will find spread wide open, 'Read your book, you yourself are enough of a reckoner against yourself this day.'" (Surah Al-Isra' 17:13-14)

The *shari'ah* of Islam grants full rights and blessings to women. Yet, in this time, you must realise that this statement of the position of women in Islam is treated as a joke by the Western world, partly through misunderstanding but, as you may know to your cost, partly through the poor impression of Islam conveyed by many Muslims themselves.

Be quite clear about one thing. It is not true Islam that impedes women, but the obstinate behaviour of so many Muslim men and women who do not fully understand what the Qur'an teaches as regards men's and women's roles, or who choose deliberately to ignore those teachings.

The Prophet Muhammad ﷺ had an enormous task when he first honoured women. It came as a severe shock to patriarchal Arab society. Try to read some of the ahadith especially those transmitted by two of the women that he ﷺ loved – Aishah ﷺ and Umm Salamah ﷺ.

Muslim men were no longer allowed (like the non-Muslims) to force widows or orphan girls to marry them. They had been doing this not for love but in order to get their hands on their inheritance money. (See Surah An-Nisa' 4:2-35 – many people do not consciously realise that the Qur'an here speaks about female orphans.)

Muslim women began to speak with boldness and freedom in the new society of Madinah. Muslim women are free individuals, Muslims who have the right to choose their marriage partners with legal and binding contracts and also the right to ask for divorce if their husbands do not prove worthy (often forgotten today – a woman can sue for divorce because of physical abuse, failure to provide adequately and for sheer incompatibility). They have the right to trade, to keep and inherit property (which remains their own within the marriage) and, in personal terms, to be treated with consideration as regards their own physical satisfaction in marriage (not just the man's) in return for their promise not to give their bodies to another man.

The Prophet Muhammad ﷺ was ordered by Allah Himself to tell all men and women that they are to do as much as they can to acquire real knowledge and better themselves and that women are as vital and important a part of the society as the men. Although it is a woman's duty to look after her man and her family as best she can and love and care for them, it is also her duty to know Allah and Islam for herself and to stand up to her husband, disobey him and obey Allah alone, if her husband is wrong in some vital matter of the *deen*.

> **"There is no obedience owed to a creature if it involves disobedience of the Creator."**
> (Hadith of Muslim)

In lesser matters she should accept his wishes out of love for him and do her best to please him and make him happy. She should accept him as the head of the household. In turn, the husband must be fair, just and reasonable in his behaviour.

People point out two things to justify ingrained ideas of the relative positions of the two sexes, so it is worth having a closer look at these.

- Firstly, the man has the right to inherit twice as much as a woman when someone dies leaving an inheritance.
- Secondly, in legal evidence the evidence of two women is taken as being equal to that of one male.

In a true Muslim society the responsibility for the maintenance of women, wives, widowed mothers, unmarried daughters and so on, falls upon men. If a woman has property or an inheritance or goes out to work, she is entitled to keep and use her own money as she wishes and is not obliged to give any of it to her husband unless she chooses to do so. The husband is obliged to be able to provide for her since she is likely to become pregnant sooner or later and unable to carry on working.

In these circumstances, and only in these, since the man carries the economic burden, it is right that his share of an inheritance should be more than that of a woman who is free to spend her money in any way she pleases. It has nothing to do with a man being double the value of a woman. For either side to exploit or put pressure on the other is an abuse of Islam.

As regards giving evidence, Qur'anic law does not require two women instead of one in any matter that requires witnesses, except in business dealings which involve contracts and in which the woman will have far less knowledge and experience than the man. It is arguable that men have greater reliability in matters involving accuracy of memory, cool judgement and the rational, rather than emotional faculties. In cases where women are just as competent as men, the witness of one woman is held to be equal to that of one man throughout the Qur'an. The whole point of these provisions is justice, to safeguard the rights of the accused, for in Islam an individual is innocent until proven guilty.

Female Islam is going through a healthy crisis as Muslim women realise that many attitudes of their people and of so-called Islamic governments are based on old cultural habits that really have nothing to do with Islam, but everything to do with people clinging to their pre-Islamic cultural patterns.

Some Muslim women have become quite militant and are making their presence felt by their zeal and fervour. They are often just as difficult to live with as male zealots who think of nothing else but shaming those around them into joining their mission groups and cliques. No doubt if a zealous man and woman can form a life partnership they may find happiness together, but they can be very overpowering for anyone who is not of like mind and can end up in very unhappy marriages. The key is moderation.

The worst tragedy is probably that in a number of cases young Muslim girls have been so harassed and pressured by men in authority over them that they have reacted violently against Islam and left the straight path, or alternatively given in and become shadowy characterless drudges, biding their time until some unknown future moment when they may be able to grasp some elusive "freedom". Some never find it and live and die in the same sorry half-state, wondering why it is that their men do not really treat them as real human beings, perhaps wondering why they themselves have not the courage to make their stand for their God-given rights.

> **"The rights of women are sacred; make sure that women are maintained in the rights assigned to them."** (Hadith of Bukhari)

What about the famous issue of women in the home? Well, women generally do the domestic work of the house for the sake of convenience, but this is not an obligation for them alone in Islam. A husband has only to study the example of the Prophet ﷺ to see how he used to help his wives with their household tasks, mend his own clothes and do manual work.

The mother is generally the one who trains the children, but it is not of the *shari'ah* either that she should be expected to carry out this extremely important and privileged task alone. It is the joint responsibility of both husband and wife to bring up their children properly and although the greater part of the daily work with the children usually falls to the wife, the husband is the principle figure of authority for the home, responsible for the welfare and behaviour of all the family members and has to set a noble example.

If you marry a good person, one who shares your values, principles and way of living, you need not fear that your life partner will not look after you or care for you or love you – or that you will not want to take on the responsibility of looking after them. This kind of loving comes naturally to all human beings; no-one wishes to live without love and everyone wants a happy and fulfilled home life.

Muslim women have the honour of knowing that Islam grants their chosen man the right to take responsibility for them when they marry.

> **"Men are responsible for women because of how Allah has favoured one over the other and because they spend from their property (for the support of women). So right-acting women are obedient, guarding in their husband's absence that which Allah has guarded."**
> (Surah An-Nisa' 4:34)

No institution works well without a clear leader and most women are quite happy for the man they love to be their leader, so long as he is worthy of respect. If the man is not worthy, she will be disappointed and rebellious, but if her chosen man is a real Muslim, then there should be no problem in accepting him as her leader with good grace. It is a Muslim man's duty to *be* worthy.

A Muslim woman should never make her man her master, however, for she has only one Master and that is Allah and she must do His will alone. This involves remembering and worshipping her Lord, knowing Islam for herself, taking care of her husband and her family, acting fairly by them and doing her duty; but she will speak out (if she is bold) or be wretchedly unhappy (if she has not got the courage to speak) if her husband does not follow the *sunnah* of the Prophet ﷺ a part of which is imitation of his loving, helpful and humble relationships with his womenfolk. She must also counsel him if he fails in the *sunnah* in other ways such as falling slack in his worship of Allah.

Creating a marriage is always a strenuous and difficult balancing act but it is one of the most worthwhile and joyful causes of all as a part of your commitment to Islam. In fact it is a very important part of your commitment, for, as you saw earlier, the Prophet ﷺ declared it to be half of the Islamic way of life.

Some Muslim men need reminding that women are not their servants, nurses, mothers, secretaries, cooks and cleaners, gardeners, shopping-trolleys, decorators and delightful sleeping partners, for nothing. This only applies if they are providers, protectors, comforters, helpers, fathers, guides, managers, chauffeurs and also make the effort to be delightful sleeping partners, too.

We need to take a good, long gentle look at our own parents' marriage relationships and learn from them. Maybe our parents have had a very good marriage or maybe not. It is important for young people to realise that many marriages go wrong because adults seem to develop a blind spot when it comes to the needs of their spouses.

Research shows that when marriages fail and end in divorce, very often one of the partners has completely lost sight of the other as a person in their own right. They think of the other only as "wife" or "husband", only in terms of how the other relates to them or what they do for them. Quite often they have no real idea of the other's likes and dislikes, opinions, interests or else simply and rather rudely regard them as of no importance.

This does not mean, of course, that every man and woman has to be perfect. Nobody is perfect, not even you. Every marriage will have its good times and bad times, its joys and distresses – but so long as we remain true to ourselves, respect our partners and share our values and principles so that our marriages are something more than a domestic and sexual arrangement, our marriages should withstand all the inevitable knocks.

Don't Be a
Religious Snob

Finally, we need to be very aware of the subtle ways in which human beings can be tempted away from real Islam by their own self-righteous concepts of "piety" which are really just a form of conceit. Maybe you have known people like this – extremely religious, but somehow their company always makes you feel guilty, depressed or bored. These are warning signs that something is wrong. The company of the Prophet ﷺ never drove people away.

Many times these pious people experience conflict and disappointment in their lives, because somehow their interpretation of love for Allah has come in between them and their love for their families, their communities and society at large. They have such high and inflexible expectations. In his lifetime, the Prophet ﷺ was very concerned about some of his followers, whom he had to remind that the best of them were those who were best to their families. Sometimes the message doesn't sink in.

It is easy for people to claim that they love Allah – they do not see Him or hear Him, and He is not going to manifest and contradict them. If someone claims to love Allah, but has great difficulty in loving or respecting the human beings around them whom they *can* see and relate to, then we have a right to be a little suspicious of their claim. Or, at least, to suspect that something has gone wrong with their Islam.

Here's an example – a parent or wife is ill or upset and in distress, but such a one knows it is time to go off to the mosque, perhaps to be away all evening. Is this Muslim right or wrong to go? He will no doubt argue that he is putting Allah first, putting Him before his family and may even produce ahadith to prove that he is right. Is this really what Allah wants?

Certainly Allah obliges this Muslim to perform the prayer, preferably with other men, but He also requires that he care for his family – and in this example his so-called devotions deprive his family and make them suffer. There is nothing to stop him from praying at home occasionally. The Muslim who neglects his or her human commitments for the sake of earning points for his or her soul has forgotten that there will be a day when all our books are opened and does not realise that perhaps their book will record clearly that they failed those whom they should have been loving and helping when they were needed by them.

Sometimes, by really putting Allah first, we have to do something for a member of our family, or a neighbour, or a fellow citizen of your town, or a stranger travelling through, or a parent, or a child, or an orphan, or a widowed or divorced woman completely outside the family. Don't forget, prayers never get in the way of love; sometimes people go to the mosque in the manner of pre-Islamic superstition or just to have the pleasure of the company of friends and not for the sake of Allah and hope for His mercy. If this is a Muslim's motivation, then perhaps you can see that he or she will perhaps be losing points for having a selfish motivation and not gaining.

It may be that women, who nearly always pray at home, understand this better than some men. What about their "points"? Well, a woman's prayer is best done at home in a secluded part of the house. The man's struggle is to "establish the prayer" in his society, but there is a danger, that in making the mosque like a men's club, the man's performance of the prayer there is really the enjoyment of the club atmosphere of men together. Who knows? It is a very dangerous thing to harbour bad opinions about people and to pass judgement on them.

Husbands, wives, parents, children of our own – all will claim our time and our love and if we wish to find happiness (which is what Allah revealed Islam for), then we must love and respect them in return and see to their needs. We must strike a balance. We must also work out when the loved one's need is truly genuine or whether they are really only just tempting us.

In cases of genuine need, most wives would probably agree that when they find their men are prepared to make sacrifices for them, there is nothing they will not sacrifice for their part. This is the nature of reality in the family and in the wider world as well. The Prophet ﷺ referred in a famous hadith to the Muslims as being "like two hands washing". When a husband and wife really care for each other, they appreciate each other and are prepared to make sacrifices for each other. The Prophet ﷺ said:

> **"The best of you is the one who is best to his family."** (Hadith of Bukhari)

Muslim women have also to pay attention to this hadith and be kind to their husbands, their children, their parents and grandparents and indeed anyone who needs their help and support. As we have noted, Allah, in the Qur'an has drawn every Muslim's attention, male or female, to the needs of all of humanity starting with the immediate members of the family but definitely not stopping with them. Indeed a Muslim, man or woman, is best recognised by their unselfish care and concern for others.

It is easy to claim that we love Allah – anybody can do that; but Muslims have to show it. This we cannot do by putting on airs or trying to give a superior impression. We should not exaggerate in our practices. Some of us seem to think that Allah will be more impressed if we make double the number of *rak'at* sometimes, rather than being regular with what is required of us. What counts with Allah is our intention, our motivation. If we continue to pray after the required amount for no reason other than our love of Allah, then we must hide it from people so that no-one ever knows about it but Allah and we will have nothing but good. However if we are merely gathering points or, disaster of disasters, want to be thought of as particularly holy and devout persons, then these are definitely bad motives.

Muslims show their regard for Allah, firstly by sacrificing themselves in doing their regular worship and, secondly, by demonstrating in action that they care for others besides themselves. It is about balancing the rights of Allah with the rights of other people.

If a parent says he or she loves a child, but then neglects it, ignores it and does nothing simply for the sake of loving it, then no matter how many times they might declare that they love it, we would not believe them. If someone says they love gardening, but never waters the plants when they see they are dying of thirst, we would not believe them. It is the same with the claim to love Allah. If someone really loves Allah, they never need to say so, they don't need to – it is the most obvious thing about them. The love they have for Allah's creatures radiates out of them.

Sometimes people develop a rather irritating habit of "preachifying", becoming religious snobs and looking down their noses at those they consider are not living up to their own high standards. This never delivers Allah's message; rather it drives people away from Allah. There is nothing to be gained from becoming over-zealous missionaries.

The best way to draw others towards Allah is to be embodiments of Islam ourselves – to make sure of our own standards and life and get on with it quietly, humbly and cheerfully. If Allah honours us, then our examples will be seen by others as the meaning of lives lived in dedication to Allah. Don't become obnoxious to others. The way of setting a good example is attractive and others will be drawn to Allah by us, insha'Allah.

In an environment like this society, where Muslims are in a minority, there can be a very dangerous tendency to turn in on ourselves and not only create a ghetto atmosphere, shutting out everyone outside the limited circle of "our own" whether that be the family or the wider community, but also a kind of race to be the most pious. Sadly, when this competitiveness enters in, the reality of Muslim brotherhood and sisterhood seems to be the first thing to go out of the door.

Some enthusiastic but divisive sectarians believe that they are the righteous ones and may even believe they are the only ones on the right path. This in itself is the surest sign of the weakness of their Islam, for it is the mark of the real Muslim that he or she will question his or her own sincerity before other people's.

On the other hand it is always sheer joy to be in the company of a genuinely saintly Muslim person – they radiate such gentleness and serenity that their beautiful and humble manner encourages us to strive to be like them, even if we cannot approach within a hundred miles of their wonderful conduct. We have to draw close to these people as much as we can.

A final point which may seem minor is that of dress. A glance at the attire worn by Muslim women in our communities will reveal an enormous range of cultural differences – from the plain, self-effacing Iranian black *chador*, to the glittering Pakistani in *shalwar qameez* and sequinned *dopatta*. If you glance further afield to Sudan, to the countries along the Silk Route and to Malaysia, you would find a wonderful diversity of ways in which Muslim women dress in modest, and usually pleasant, fashion. Similarly with men, the crisp, white robes of the Arabs, long shirts and trousers of other peoples, the waistwrapper of the Malays, the turbans, haiks, caps and hats; there is a wonderful variety of ways of conforming to the *sunnah* of modesty.

You may have your own personal opinions on these styles of dress; but you must realise that the clothes any of these Muslims wear are no indication whatsoever of how good or true their Islam is. Anyone wearing a particular style of dress as a badge proclaiming themselves as *Islamic* (it is important to understand the difference between being a Muslim, one submitted to Allah, and being *Islamic*), those not doing it being, by implication, less than *Islamic* or *un-Islamic*, then their attitude is not really one becoming of a Muslim. It is the very opposite of modesty – it is showing off.

Being a Muslim always involves challenge and thought. We have to be consciously aware of ourselves and our motives all the time and, in this way, we become involved in changing ourselves and the society in which we live for the better.

Be Yourself

One of the most important matters to cling on to is the realisation of your great importance for the future. Parents and elders sometimes have a tendency to forget about this – foolishly as it happens. Few politicians ever forget it. Few businessmen running thriving companies ever forget it. Existing voters, customers and the workforce grow older day by day and whether these grown-ups like to admit it or not, there will come a time when they will have to move over and make way for you – the next generation.

What your generation will be like is to a certain extent dependent on the ways in which the older generation have moulded you – and that is one reason why parents and teachers are always so eager to develop young people in their charge along certain lines. However, you know (often to your own cost) that parents and teachers are not always of the highest standards themselves and the well meant plans that others make for you and your friends and acquaintances often go completely awry.

We also discover, as we get older, that frequently the senior generation see things from a different point of view from us – perhaps from the point of view of people who may once have been idealistic themselves, but who struck disaster and had to submit to experience, sometimes bitter. Elders who care for us are usually just trying a few shortcuts, trying to save us from making the same mistakes they made – but sometimes people cannot learn this way.

There's an old proverb – "the fool learns from his own mistakes, but the wise person learns from the mistakes of others". Sadly, when it comes to living, most of us need to make our own mistakes and few of us really learn from observing other people. We may think we are clever – but all too often we are really fools and need to learn the humility to see it. (Needless to say, everyone else spots it long before we do.)

Being a Muslim is a very public business. The act of entering Islam (*shahadah*) and all the important pillars are performed where possible in public, particularly by the men. Our actions will be witnessed by many people. There are our nearest and dearest (often our most discerning critics – they know us stripped of all pretence and disguise); there are all the people we will come to meet and interact with, those we will like and those we will dislike; there are our recording angels, poised to write every wrong deed (but quick to erase it if we regret it and turn away from it) and also poised to note down each little success. There is Allah, the Exalted, Himself, in whose hands are our very lives, the Ultimate Witness and a Compassionate One, over our deeds and even our inmost thoughts.

We may have had Muslim upbringings in good homes and attended good mosques, but what we have heard and observed is useless to us unless we believe and affirm it and act on it for ourselves. However much our parents may wish us to become believing Muslims, they cannot do this for us, on our behalf, because each one of us has to make our own response (answer) to Allah – first hand. We cannot be second-hand Muslims. As one person put it, "You say you were born in a Muslim home. So what? If a cat has kittens in the oven, does that make them biscuits?"

We might imagine that when we start off as self-motivating Muslims, that we might feel lonely at first, or isolated, wondering if anyone else really feels as we do. We are not alone at all – very many people feel just the same as we do, even if we don't at present know them. When we pray in the Muslim way, this is one way to end our isolation. It doesn't matter whether we are praying alone or with other people (although it is better that we pray with others, particularly for men) – we are not alone, for Allah and His angels draw very close to us at these times. Moreover, remember that as we face towards the Ka'bah in Makkah there are literally millions of others, men and women, young and old, from all over the earth, praying in the same way at the same time. They are people, from all sorts of different walks of life, who have many of the same dilemmas as we do, and are serious and dedicated Muslims.

Prayer is living our daily lives with Him. He is the only One we can find closer to us than our jugular veins, to Whom we can tell everything that is in us. He, of course, is always present at all the hours of the day and the night, not just at the times of the prayers even if we do not realise it. Prayer helps to make us aware of His presence, which we might not realise if we do not pay attention.

Allah is He Who knows everything about us and from Whom we receive everything. That is why we should be humble – not because we want to concentrate on our weakness or helplessness or poor talents, but a joyful humility because He is *so* great and *so* close to us and because we do not deserve His goodness to us. If Allah punished us according to what we deserve, there would be no-one left on earth. (See Surah Fatir 35:45 and Surah An-Nahl 16:61). Thankfully, Allah is not like that. He knows our weaknesses (how could He not since He created us) and when we regret our failings, He forgives us.

It does not matter if we are nobody, if we have nothing, for our lowering ourselves before Allah is what raises us up, our slavehood to Him is what sets us free. If we live simply with these certainties, we will realise more and more the reality of His presence, and we will find joy in it.

Life is given to us to learn to recognise Allah and to come to trust Him. Everything that happens, no matter how upsetting, leads the Muslim to increase in that inner quality. When things go wrong for us and we are hurt, these are the very times when we begin to see our way most clearly. How? Well, you know how people say that when it comes to the crunch, you find out who your real friends are? When you find out who your *Real* Friend is, you have lost nothing and gained everything. Whatever our difficulties and our fears of going astray, we can be sure that we are on the straight path if what happens to us teaches us to understand more and more clearly what our Path means. We belong to Allah, we are in His hands. This is the ground of all our hope and nothing can destroy this because it is beyond earthly hope.

It doesn't matter if we don't understand everything. Life is an adventurous journey of learning and discovery. If we knew everything in one go, we would have nothing left to discover. If we really trust Him, if He truly means everything to us, we have only to turn in His direction. We should offer ourselves to Him in all our weakness and insecurity, with nothing but the desire to obey Him and let Him work in us.

If we cannot express ourselves properly, it doesn't matter. Allah knows what we are trying to say and trying to do. Islam means "to submit", and Iman (faith, belief) means "to accept" and "to trust". We must accept our trials and difficulties, even upsetting ones, even ones which come from other people, perhaps from those we care most for.

We must not be hostile or superior or quick to judge or censor others. Humility towards Allah, in accepting the trials He sends us, must be part of our deepest being. Let us trust in Allah's mercy, in His faithfulness. He is always at work, in our hearts and in the creation, He never slumbers or sleeps. His mercy takes hold of every heart that really desires it, however poor and weak that heart may feel.

Allah is Who the Qur'an says He is, our Creator is communicating with us through the Qur'an and through the creation. If we do not respond we are missing the whole point of our existence. Allah speaks, so we must answer. If we are reading these words, then we know that He speaks, that there is a Messenger, that there is a Message. It would be stupid to maintain a stubborn silence pretending that we have not heard.

What kind of people does Allah show mercy to? He shows mercy to us, while we are still in wrong action, while we are still powerless and helpless, while we are still ungrateful. He shows mercy to them, while they are still ungrateful wrongdoers and, perhaps, even nasty and unpleasant to us. He knows things we do not know; He sees what we do not see. He sees their hearts and knows the reasons why they behave as they do; He sees our hearts and knows how we cope with their hostility.

Remember that Allah's mercy encompasses everything and every person. Be like that as much as you can. But remember that Allah hates wrong action, most seriously, worship of other than Him. He calls on us, if we worship and serve Him, to be at war with all wrong action and injustice, wherever we may find it, but not to forget His all-encompassing mercy, even on our enemies and His. We may love this person less than that, because we are human – but remember that Allah may see them differently. His compassion, His generosity, His freedom have no limits – His mercy surrounds every person, even those we do not like, whether they are aware of it or not. The pitiful, unpleasant, selfish, unkind, spiteful bully who keeps picking on us and spoiling our lives is also surrounded by the mercy of Allah, even if he doesn't believe in Him.

The instant that person feels sorrow and remorse and takes a faltering step towards Allah asking for help (many have done that without even knowing His name), that is the instant that Allah comes towards him or her, at the run.

If we care for Allah, then we must start modelling ourselves on some of His qualities. Sometimes humans have more compassion for animals than for other humans. We understand that a frightened, ill-treated Alsatian dog is likely to bite the hand stretched out to help it – and we accept it with a smile and carry on helping. As Muslims, we need to translate that same attitude across to distressed human beings. We have to see that they are crippled and hurt by wrong action (in all its gross and subtle forms) and not mind if they try to bite us, but still carry on helping them.

Islam is a gift, the greatest gift, from Him Whom we trust, in Whose hands are our self-forms, our souls. He Himself kindles our trust in Him within us and puts in our hearts something greater than our very hearts. Our faith would not be possible if He in Whom we trust and have confidence did not exist. Our trust in Him is the proof of Him.

Trusting Allah means knowing and saying with our whole beings that He means everything to us, knowing that nothing in our lives makes sense except in relation to Him. We may not understand, we may not be perfect, we may have limited talents and abilities, we may be tormented by doubts, fears and periods of panic, yet, you know that Allah never ceases to watch over us and show mercy to us and to Him we are returning.

May Allah bless you and keep watch over you. May you always have the comfort of knowing His merciful caring for you, and that your soul is safe in His hands.

In the Name of Allah, the Merciful, the Compassionate
"By the morning light of the forenoon,
And by the night when it is still,
Your Lord has not forsaken you
And He does not hate (you).
And truly the next life is better for you
than the first.
And certainly your Lord will give you
so that you are contented.
Did He not find you an orphan
and He sheltered (you)?
And He found you astray
and He guided (you)?
And He found you in great need
and He enriched (you)?
So, as for the orphan,
do not oppress (him).
And as for the one who asks,
do not refuse (him).
And as for the blessing of your Lord,
then declare (it).
(Surah Ad-Duha 93)